IDI AMIN AND MOAMMAR GADHAFI

Lessons from the Story Part 1

Margaret Akulia

IDI AMIN AND MOAMMAR GADHAFI

Copyright © 2011 by Margaret Akulia

All rights reserved. No part of this book may be reproduced or transmitted in any form or by any means without written permission of the author.

ISBN 9780986614934

To the people of Uganda and Libya

Acknowledgments

Chapters two to fifteen of this book are reproductions of sections of the book titled Idi Amin: Hero or Villain? His Son Jaffar Amin and Other People Speak authored by Jaffar Amin and Margaret Akulia ISBN 9780986614903.

Table of Contents

CHAPTER ONE 1

    Idi Amin: Muslim Brother or means to an end? 1

    Africa's "King of Kings", Caliph or other? 8

    The African Union and the Arab League 11

    Lessons from the story 14

CHAPTER TWO 15

    The mystical events involving Dad 15

    Dad's secret meeting in Egypt with Prince Faisal 16

    A secret meeting with a female Mossad Agent 19

    Grandma's warning for Dad 21

    Dad's realization that he had to pick sides 22

    Ploys by the descendants of Isaac and Ishmael 23

    Dad's arrival from Abdel Nasser's funeral 24

    A standing ovation and continuing events 24

CHAPTER THREE 29

    The day Dad overthrew Apollo Milton Obote 29

    "Detention Decree", foreign trips and a "plot" 34

    A short-lived "honeymoon" with Israel 35

Friendships with King Faisal and Al-Qadhafi 39

A break in the rock solid relationship with Israel........................39

Drawing the lines and "dragging" Ugandans 42

CHAPTER FOUR...43

Blood is thicker than water..43

A reflection on the relationship with the Israelis.........................44

King Faisal's gift to Dad of the Lear Jet..44

A Diplomatic Relationship with Libya 45

The Addis Ababa Agreement for Peace..48

Dad's 180-degree turn against Israel 53

CHAPTER FIVE 57

The time the last Israelis left Uganda 57

Rumours of a coup and a return from a Tour 58

Friendships with African leaders and an agenda 59

Support for the Ummah and consolidating Islam 65

CHAPTER SIX...75

Dad's 1973 "Dream Speech" at the OAU 75

A champion for causes 80

The 1974 French Film Documentary on Dad.................................84

CHAPTER SEVEN..87

Events in neighbouring countries and a coup 87

The sentence to death of Denis Hills 95

CHAPTER EIGHT 103

Dad as Chairman of the OAU 103

"Black Empowerment" and Arab Groups 105

Fond memories of the bald Black American 106

A spear throwing jest with American friends 108

An inversion of roles 110

Relishing the opportunity to showcase Uganda 111

Dad's clarity at the 1975 OAU Summit 113

Addressing the UN and Resolution 3379 114

CHAPTER NINE 119

A tussle between bodyguards and an Assassin 119

Support and preparation for UN Resolution 3379 120

Dad's medals, honours and opposition to Israel 121

Opening Uganda House in New York and a tip 123

"Economic War" and an unusual encounter 125

The chickens associated with opposition to Israel 130

The "Raid" on Entebbe by Israelis 131

CHAPTER TEN 135

A "Conversation" with Major General Lumago 135

Being "taunted" after the "Raid" 136

A 180-degree turn and our Jewish siblings 137

A prayer for a Jewish-Muslim Peace Pact 143

How Dad became entangled in the "Raid" 144

Singing a "Gospel Song" for Dad 145

Dad's naughty jest on the British Royal Family 148

CHAPTER ELEVEN 151

The war between Uganda and Tanzania 151

An unnerving phone call to Dad about the war 158

The death of Lieutenant Colonel Godwin Sule 159

At the frontline waving at the Tanzanian Forces 162

CHAPTER TWELVE 165

"Part One Order" to repatriate families 165

Allegations that Dad's army had been bought off 168

Our rescue by a Platoon 169

Our last days in Uganda 176

CHAPTER THIRTEEN.. 183

The day my family fled to Libya in a Cargo Plane 183

The time Dad's Presidential Guards waylaid him...................... 185

- Dad's last emotional speech 186
- The fall of Kampala and celebrations 188
- Dad running the gauntlet on the way to safety 194

CHAPTER FOURTEEN 199

- A special Libyan C-130 Hercules Plane 199
- Our first days in Libya 203
- An indecent pass by a Libyan Bodyguard 204
- Relocating to the Kingdom of Saudi Arabia 206
- Dad as a devout Muslim and a Training 208
- Our Boxing and Kung Fu Training 210
- A Typical day at our household in Saudi Arabia 212

CHAPTER FIFTEEN 215

- Our Spiritual experiences in Saudi Arabia 215
- A visit in Saudi Arabia from our uncle 218
- Running into Nation of Islam's Louis Farrakhan 221
- Islam's benign presence in our family 226

CHAPTER ONE

Idi Amin: Muslim Brother or means to an end?

"While we lived in Libya, a rift developed between Dad and Al-Qadhafi following Al-Qadhafi's close association with Julius Nyerere while trying to gain the OAU (Organization of African Unity) seat that year 1979. Dad viewed Al-Qadhafi's close association with Julius Nyerere as betrayal. So, in characteristic defiance, he dramatically insisted on walking all the way to Makkah (Mecca) if Al-Qadhafi did not offer him safe passage to the Kingdom of Saudi Arabia."

Those were the words of Idi Amin's son Jaffar Amin as I engaged him and other people in candid "conversation" about his father Idi Amin's legacy which we outline in a series titled, <u>Idi Amin: Hero or Villain? His Son Jaffar Amin and Other People Speak</u>. The series is devoted to uncovering Idi Amin's story in its entirety, layer by layer, telling all the truth and shedding light on the untruths and Moammar Gadhafi features very prominently in the story.

A combined force of the Tanzania Peoples' Defence Force and Ugandan exiles operating through Tanzania had ousted Idi Amin from power in Uganda on April 11, 1979 after Moammar Gadhafi sent Libyan troops to fight against

Tanzania on behalf of Idi Amin. Moammar Gadhafi had also been the person who whisked Idi Amin out of Uganda in a special Libyan plane after Idi Amin's government was overthrown.

On April 23, 1979, a Libyan C-130 Hercules landed at Arua Airstrip where Idi Amin had retreated to. While there, he had continued broadcasting from a local radio station and telling Ugandans that he was still in power. It was from this location that Moammar Gadhafi was able to whisk Idi Amin out of harm's way to Libya, as the opposition forces who eventually ousted him closed in on his government.

"I recall that Dad arrived in Benghazi on April 23, 1979 from our Arua Tanganyika Aerodrome aboard the C130 Hercules Transporter that Al-Qadhafi sent to pick him up after his government was overthrown. We had a tearful reunion with Dad on April 24, 1979 in Tripoli, Libya" Jaffar Amin recounted of the time his father arrived in Libya after he had sent his children and one of his wives ahead while he continued to fight for control of Uganda as the world watched his government crumble.

After Idi Amin's government was overthrown in Uganda, Moammar Gadhafi welcomed him and his entourage into Libya where the Libyan government took care of them for several months. On the little known occasion relating to Idi Amin threatening to walk to the Kingdom of

Saudi Arabia if Moammar Gadhafi did not offer him safe passage to the holy land of Sunni Islam, Idi Amin had felt betrayed by Moammar Gadhafi because Moammar Gadhafi wanted to be the Chairman of the OAU (Organization of African Unity) in 1979. To increase his chances of getting elected to the Chairmanship of the OAU, Moammar Gadhafi had to "befriend" Julius Nyerere, the President of Tanzania who was responsible for Idi Amin's ouster from power in Uganda.

Following the betrayal felt by Idi Amin, he relocated to the Kingdom of Saudi Arabia which had bestowed on him the highest honour in Islam during his rule in Uganda. Saudi Arabia considered Idi Amin a champion of Islam during his rule in Uganda and rewarded him for that championship. One of the rewards was a 1972 special trip to Uganda by King Faisal Bin Abdul Aziz Al-Saud, the King of Saudi Arabia at the time.

"The trip was a rare gesture by the king and his only known trip to Sub-Saharan Africa" offered Jaffar as he told of this unprecedented visit by the King of Saudi Arabia to a Sub-Saharan African country.

The irony was that it was Moammar Gadhafi who had funded some of the "lucrative" rewards that came with Idi Amin's championship to advance Islam. However, notwithstanding the large gifts he received from Moammar Gadhafi, Saudi Arabia also "showered" Idi Amin with additional gifts when he followed through with suggestions to end a rock solid relationship he once had with Israel and support the Ummah (Community of Muslim Believers) instead.

Accepting the "lucrative" rewards from Moammar Gadhafi and the Saudi Royal Family placed Idi Amin at the epicenter of the Arab-Israeli Conflict. Being at the epicenter of this conflict would create the domino effect that led to a hostage-rescue mission commonly known as "The Entebbe Raid" which was undertaken by the Israeli Elite Special Forces in 1976, to rescue Israeli hostages held by pro-Palestinian hijackers at Entebbe Airport in Uganda, East Africa. It would also create a domino effect for Uganda and Idi Amin himself and lead to some of the events outlined in the series titled, <u>Idi Amin: Hero or Villain? His Son Jaffar Amin and Other People Speak</u>.

The OAU (Organisation of African Unity) that Moammar Gadhafi wanted to head was a body established in 1963 for the primary purpose of promoting unity and solidarity among African countries. In 2002, it was replaced by the African Union which Moammar Gadhafi was instrumental in conceiving while pursuing and funding the idea of a United States of Africa. The United States of Africa is the proposed name for a unified Africa comprising a federation of African countries.

It would be thirty years later in the year 2009 that Moammar Gadhafi would finally be elected Chairman of the African Union, which replaced the OAU (Organization of African Unity). That year, Moammar Gadhafi got his wish to lead the African Institution at last!

Prior to Moammar Gadhafi's election as Chairman of the African Union in February 2009, a group of African traditional rulers and kings bestowed on him the title "King of Kings", in preparation for his assumed role as the leader of the United States of Africa. The lavish ceremony was held in Benghazi, Libya in 2008 and it was funded by Moammar Gadhafi himself. It was followed by a February 1, 2009 coronation ceremony in Addis Ababa, Ethiopia that coincided with the African Union Summit on February 2, 2009, during which Moammar Gadhafi was elected head of the African Union for the year 2009.

Idi Amin and Moammar Gadhafi became "friends" in 1972 when Moammar Gadhafi told him to end a rock solid relationship Idi Amin once had with Israel and support the Arab people instead. However, some critics insist that for Moammar Gadhafi, the "friendship" with Idi Amin was just a means to an end because he wanted to score a point against Israel in the ongoing Arab-Israeli Conflict while aiming to be the King of the entire continent of Africa in the long run. They assert that when Moammar Gadhafi used the "Muslim Card" to get Idi Amin to do his "bidding," he did not consider Idi Amin a Muslim Brother at all but a means to an end.

According to Jaffar Amin, two years before his father Idi Amin and Moammar Gadhafi became friends, King Faisal Bin Abdul Aziz Al-Saud of Saudi Arabia asked Idi Amin a typically provocative Muslim Question during a secret meeting they had in Egypt while attending Egyptian President Gamal Abdel Nasser's funeral in 1970.

"You call yourself a Muslim Eid Al-Amin when you as Army Commander let your land be used for Zionist Hegemony over the Arab Muslim Nations in Africa and the Middle East? Have you ever sat down and asked yourself why Uganda would need a sixteen capacity simultaneous takeoff runway, for F4 Phantom Jets on your land, if not but to be a southern hemisphere rear base to enable the illegitimate Jewish state to attack Arab Muslim countries from the southern Hemisphere? Ask yourself sincerely……"

Idi Amin ended the rock solid relationship he once had with Israel in 1972 and became involved in the Arab-Israeli Conflict. Needless to say, Israel felt deeply betrayed by him. The break in the relationship was what precipitated the hostage-rescue mission commonly known as "The Entebbe Raid" that played itself out in Uganda in 1976. The hostage-rescue mission cost Uganda

CHAPTER ONE

precious lives and set off more of the events outlined in the series titled, <u>Idi Amin: Hero or Villain? His Son Jaffar Amin and Other People Speak</u>.

Notwithstanding the critics' assertions in relation to Idi Amin and Moammar Gadhafi, Idi Amin ruled the East African country of Uganda from January 25, 1971 to April 11, 1979 and left a controversial and conflicted legacy, as depicted in various movies including "The Last King of Scotland" starring Oscar-winning film star Forest Whitaker and Raid on Entebbe, a 1977 TV movie based on the hostage-rescue mission undertaken by the Israeli Elite Special Forces in 1976, to rescue Israeli hostages held by pro-Palestinian hijackers at Entebbe Airport in Uganda, East Africa.

On that occasion, an Air France Flight 139 originating in Tel Aviv, Israel had been hijacked by two members of the Popular Front for the Liberation of Palestine and two Germans from the Revolutionary Cells. The plane is reported to have landed in Uganda after a refueling stop in Benghazi, Libya, because Idi Amin had become fully involved in the Arab-Israeli Conflict by that time and Moammar Gadhafi urged him to allow the plane to land in Uganda.

Critics have persisted in their assertions that Moammar Gadhafi had many "hidden agendas" when he initiated his "friendship" with Idi Amin in 1972. They claim that these "hidden agendas" included eventually ruling the entire continent of Africa as an Islamic Caliphate under sharia law. They maintain that Moammar Gadhafi successfully merged several of these "hidden agendas" when he and Idi Amin signed and issued a Joint Communiqué in Tripoli, Libya, on February 14, 1972 that declared unwavering support for Arab Peoples.

"The two Heads of State undertake to conduct themselves according to the precepts of Islam. They assure their support to the Arab peoples in their struggle against Zionism and Imperialism for the liberation of confiscated lands and for the right of the Palestine people to return to their land and homes by all means" the Communiqué read in part.

Africa's "King of Kings", Caliph or other?

Jaffar Amin recalls the year they spent in Libya and his father's decision to relocate to the Kingdom of Saudi Arabia. Of the day his father threatened to walk to the Kingdom of Saudi Arabia if Moammar Gadhafi didn't offer him passage, he writes:

"When Dad felt a year's stay in Libya was long enough for him, he actually walked a distance of almost 5,000+ metres before he was convinced by Ugandan Diplomats, Ministers and his Personal Bodyguards to gracefully return to the hotel complex in the official car. The car had trailed the former Head of State along the whole way. This was the same hotel complex where our family and Dad's entourage had been accommodated from the time Dad landed in Libya after his government was overthrown in Uganda. The Great Libyan Leader finally relented and placed Dad, our family and an entourage of over 80 people on a flight to the Kingdom of Saudi Arabia. So, in 1980 we relocated to Jeddah, Saudi Arabia."

Regarding Jaffar Amin's reference to Moammar Gadhafi as "The Great Leader", the title originates from the fact that despite reports that Moammar Gadhafi funded "terrorism" and "terrorist activities", many people in Africa forgave him because of his "generosity" and considered him a "Great Leader". Libya's vast oil wealth enabled Moammar Gadhafi to mediate conflicts in Africa, sponsor the spread of Islam on the African continent, fund the African Union and his idea of a United States of Africa and give out large amounts of humanitarian assistance.

However, critics are quick to suggest that he fueled some of the same conflicts he "mediated." They also maintain that Moammar Gadhafi used Libyan oil money to "buy" the title of Africa's "King of Kings" and he planned to use the title to accomplish the "hidden agendas" he had when he "befriended" Idi Amin in 1972.

Nonetheless, because of the "honourable" gestures of mediating conflicts in Africa, sponsoring the spread of Islam on the African continent, funding the African Union, funding his "honourable" idea of a United States of Africa and giving out large amounts of humanitarian assistance, Moammar Gadhafi was forgiven by many Africans who felt that he had earned the title of "The Great Leader" in some way. They had "looked the other way" and even gone along with his use of the title Africa's "King of Kings" until the horrific images of the full-scale February 2011 revolt by the people of Libya.

According to reports, Moammar Gadhafi reiterated his title of Africa's "King of Kings" at the 2009 Arab League Summit held on Monday, March 30, 2009 while proclaiming that he was also the Leader of the Arab Leaders and the Imam of the Muslims.

"I am the leader of the Arab leaders, the king of kings of Africa and the imam of the Muslims," Moammar Gadhafi is quoted to have proclaimed during the 2009 Arab League Summit where it is reported that he also insulted King Abdullah of Saudi Arabia, the custodian of the holy land of Sunni Islam and assumed Caliph of the Islamic Ummah.

Exactly who was Moammar Gadhafi before the full-scale February 2011 revolt by the people of

Libya? Was he Africa's "King of Kings", Caliph of the Islamic Ummah or something else?

The African Union and the Arab League

Libya and many parts of the Middle East "went up in flames" exactly thirty-nine years to the day Idi Amin and Moammar Gadhafi signed and issued the Joint Communiqué in Tripoli, Libya, on February 14, 1972 that declared unwavering support for Arab Peoples. As the International Community continues to grapple with answers to the never ending "Middle East Problem", some of the answers may lie in lessons offered by Idi Amin and Moammar Gadhafi's story.

The intended outcome of the Joint Communiqué they signed in 1972 was to "merge" the agendas of the Arab League and the Organisation of African Unity (OAU) and Moammar Gadhafi appears to have accomplished this outcome on the surface. However, critics have been consistent in reproaching the two institutions for "standing on the sidelines" in efforts to "clean up" "messes" created by their members in Africa and the Middle East.

They argue that the need for these two institutions to "walk their talks" and provide effective leadership in dealing with unruly and murderous leaders in their midst became more pronounced with the full-scale February 2011 revolt by the people of Libya against Moammar Gadhafi.

Critics insist that the African Union and the Arab League should lead "fights" against their members who "refuse to step down" and massacre their way to power so that these "leaders" don't use the "colonialism and racism cards" to "cripple" global intervention for purposes of continuing to stay in power.

In response to the institutions' tendencies to just "parrot" resolutions and take no action, critics scold that their leadership in resolving "African and Middle East Problems" should not just be "lip service" either. Consequently, a closer look at how the African Union and the Arab League should have averted the massacres that occurred in Libya and what they must do in similar situations is critical.

A statement Moammar Gadhafi is reported to have made as he vowed to crash the opposition is further indication that the African Union and the Arab League could have prevented the massacre of Libyans. This is because the statement alludes to Moammar Gadhafi's dependence on the populations the two institutions represent for his survival.

"I am in the middle of the people in the Green Square. ... This is the people that loves Moammar Gadhafi. If the people of Libya and the

Arabs and Africans don't love Moammar Gadhafi then Moammar Gadhafi does not deserve to live."

Moammar Gadhafi realized that he had to "fight to the death" because he needed Libya's vast resources to continue being the "Leader and Guide of the Revolution of Libya", "King of Kings" of Africa, "Leader of the Arab Leaders" and the "Imam of the Muslims." However, the answers to three critical questions will determine how the global community handles the fate of others around the world who might find themselves in a similar situation to Libyans.

Should it be "business as usual" with leaders in Africa, the Middle East and other parts of the world who massacre their way to power?

How can the African Union and the Arab League "step up to the plate", "walk their talks" and stop their members from massacring civilians to continue hanging onto power?

What is needed to enable the people of the world to act immediately instead of "standing by" when citizens of countries around the world are being slaughtered by the people who are supposed to protect them?

The answers to the above questions may determine who becomes an accomplice to mass murder.

Lessons from the story

<u>Idi Amin and Moammar Gadhafi: Lessons from the Story</u> takes a close look at the lessons offered by Idi Amin and Moammar Gadhafi's story in light of events in the Middle East and Africa and the February 2011 revolts by Libyan people against Moammar Gadhafi.

Aimed at learning and teaching from the story, Part 1 comprises of sections of the book titled <u>Idi Amin: Hero or Villain? His Son Jaffar Amin and Other People Speak</u> (ISBN 9780986614903) which relate to Moammar Gadhafi. The sections are reproduced as chapters two to fifteen for purposes of providing context.

Part 2 and subsequent parts will include the Al-Qaeda and Muslim Brotherhood connection to Idi Amin and Moammar Gadhafi's story and related events.

CHAPTER TWO

The mystical events involving Dad

While Dad was in Egypt attending Abdel Nasser's funeral, a couple of "mystical" events occurred in relation to the age old "fight" between the descendants of Abraham's children Isaac and Ishmael and Dad unwittingly became a pawn. The "mystical" events were connected to Dad's very strong relationship with Israel at the time while also being part of the Ummah (Community of Muslim Believers). The events unfolded right before Dad's eyes like a scene out of a Hollywood movie and he was both "tickled" and overwhelmed by them.

According to Dad, as Obote and his entourage continued to "scheme" and "craft" a plot to get rid of him in his absence, Mossad Agents were "secretly" clocking their every move and putting a few plans in action. Dad claimed that the Israeli Mossad duly sent a Female Agent who flew in from New York as part of the Press Corps to cover the Funeral of Abdel Nasser to warn Dad and convey instructions from "higher up". According to Dad, unbeknownst to him, he had been earmarked for leadership by the Judeo Western powers that be as early as 1963 when he went for Paratrooper Training in the Jewish Holy Land and by 1964 following the Uganda Rifles (UR) Mutiny at the 1st Battalion King George IV Barracks Jinja.

The "mystical" events that unraveled while Dad was in Egypt attending Abdel Nasser's funeral are little known in the public domain but they were what Dad would reminisce about that Autumn (Fall) season endlessly at the dinner table at our Al Safa Residence in Saudi Arabia. The events would have far reaching repercussions on the revolutionary transition from Abdel Nasser to his eventual successor and rubble rouser from the most unexpected of corners in the African and Middle Eastern region at large.

According to Dad, the Mossad followed his every move. However, unbeknownst to their Agents, two singular events took place secretly in relation to the Ummah (Community of Muslim Believers) while he was in Egypt.

Dad's secret meeting in Egypt with Prince Faisal

During an informal gathering that occurred within the course of the day in the vicinity of the mosque after our obligatory five prayers, Crown Prince Faisal Bin Abdul Aziz expressed and admired and indeed intimated to Dad great admiration. He conveyed to Dad that he was proud of the fact that a Muslim was the Head of the Military Establishment in Uganda which was a predominantly Christian Country. During this first meeting, Crown Prince Faisal Bin Abdul Aziz arranged for another secret meeting to take place between him and Dad before his departure for Jeddah after the Funeral of Gamal Abdel Nasser.

According to Dad, he was greatly affected and moved by the insight and keen interest shown by the de facto King of Saudi Arabia in the ongoing build up and frenzied Zionist operations in Uganda and the Sudan. When he addressed the issue with Dad, a frenzied construction of a state of the art large haulage Airbase was taking place at Nakasongola Military Air Base in Uganda - dead centre in the heart of Africa. Realization came thick and fast as the King asked Dad a typically provocative Muslim Question:

"You call yourself a Muslim Eid Al-Amin when you as Army Commander let your land be used for Zionist Hegemony over the Arab Muslim Nations in Africa and the Middle East? Have you ever sat down and asked yourself why Uganda would need a sixteen capacity simultaneous takeoff runway, for F4 Phantom Jets on your land, if not but to be a southern hemisphere rear base to enable the illegitimate Jewish state to attack Arab Muslim countries from the southern Hemisphere? Ask yourself sincerely......"

Perplexed, Dad said he sat back and reflected on the revelation since he had often wondered at the astronomically Juggernaut construction activity that continued apace in Nakasongola

Military Airbase unabated by economic woes or Uganda's incapacity to afford such a White Elephant project. Moreover Uganda did not have the financial clout and only had miniscule Israeli Fuga Jets and Bombers. The notion of what purpose the Airbase would be for had continued to cross his mind so this insight by King Designate Faisal Bin Abdul Aziz put his mind to rest.

Alas on hindsight today the Airbase has been turned into a Bullets Munitions Factory manned by North Koreans and the very Dad was lambasted by the very Western media for building a "White Elephant deep in the middle of nowhere".

The King continued to forcefully place the seed of his Islamic Agenda on schedule to a willing fellow Muslim. When he felt Dad was open to his wise suggestions and the effects of the revelations were indeed succeeding, he asked Dad to realize his great potential as a Muslim Leader and Muslims should always work together he intimated. Then he added, "And we should always show allegiance to our creed and defend the Ummah".

The Dye had been cast and it was to be sealed some two years into the future on King Faisal's only travel to Sub-Saharan Africa on his momentous visit to Uganda. It would bring an end to Dad's perception by Israel as a Reliable Helmsman (HAGAI NE'EMAN). This would happen despite a second revelation and another event that is not in the public arena relating to the female Mossad Agent allegedly flown from New York to warn Dad and convey instructions from "higher up" in order to continue solidifying his relationship with Israel.

A secret meeting with a female Mossad Agent

According to Dad, he met up with the female Mossad Agent who had come specifically from New York to inform him of the intended plans of Obote against him while he was in the land of the Pharaohs attending the funeral of a descendant of Abraham's son Ishmael. What an unbelievable sequence of events!

"Just as I alighted at my official hotel following the funeral service of Gamal Abdel Nasser, I was cordially accosted by an enchanting Mediterranean lady of unspecified origins, who requested for a private meeting" Dad told.

Intrigued by the beautiful lady's interest in him Dad accepted and invited her for dinner. He was baited when she claimed to have been sent by Colonel Baruch Balev an intimate chum of Dad's at the time who had been instrumental in coordinating all cordial military activity and bilateral relationships between Israel and the 1st Republic of Uganda since 1963. That had also been the year Dad was promoted to the rank of Major and sent for a tour of the defense facilities in the Judeo State. Dad later attended a Paratrooper Training in the Judeo Holy Land as well.

The beautiful lady intimated to Dad that she was sent on an urgent mission from New York to meet him and convey an urgent message from Colonel Balev. She told Dad that his life was in danger and that Obote was rearranging the High Rank military structure so he should urgently return to Uganda but he was not to use the direct route to Entebbe. The beautiful lady said Dad should head via Gulu Airbase, which had a strong presence of Israeli Trainers. They were training the Ugandan Pilots on the Vector tail winged Fuga Jet Fighters/Bombers.

According to Dad, he received instructions for the DC4 (DAKOTA) to first land in Gulu before continuing to Entebbe Airport possibly via the Jinja Airstrip. Dad said he was to continue to Entebbe Airport after meeting and getting a briefing from Israeli Military Instructors who would guide his every movement from the time he touched down in the country. The beautiful lady told Dad that Obote was intending to accuse and finalize the implication of the murder of Brigadier General Okoya and the loss of funds from the Uganda Ministry of Defense Coffers towards funding his Mabira Units training and armament which was unearthed by Aggrey Awori.

Dad was momentarily dumbfounded by the enormous political interest in his person from all corners of the geo-Political Protagonists. Being at the very epicenter both alarmed and tickled his enormous ego, while he continued to listen to this petite Guardian Angel sent from God's Chosen People as his late mother Aisha Aate Chumaru was fond of calling Moshe's People. It was interesting how Dad's kid brother Adinebi Amin was given the name Moshe too, when he went for Battle Tank Training in Israel.

Grandma's warning for Dad

Dad had reflected over the "mystical" events that unfolded in Egypt while sadly recalling the events of the last year 1969 when Grandma died around mid August. That time, the Israeli Paratroopers' Regiment sent a team specially from Israel with a garland of flowers which was parachuted over Arua Town trailing colours of smoke with deft accuracy. There was also a lone Paratrooper who landed exactly next to Grandma Aisha's grave near Masjid Noor on Rhino Camp Road and placed the garland of flowers on her grave. It was a technical marvel to all that witnessed the event apart from the one event involving another Paratrooper who was supposed to land at Dad's residence some one mile away from Grandma's grave. This Paratrooper overshot and landed on the roof of Mzee Doka's House just across the Jiako road at Tanganyika Village, Arua instead. A multitude had gathered at Mzee Doka's house for Grandma's funeral and witnessed the strange spectacle, which became a talking point for a long time.

The above show of sympathy and support was a strong bonding which Colonel Baruch Balev knew would touch the soul of this stern but simple Kakwa Soldier he had learnt to respect despite most people's under estimation of his potential and he genuinely held Dad in high esteem. Now here he was again in 1970, scheming and directing his life and destiny towards Power and Dominion.

As the "mystical" events were unfolding right before Dad's eyes, he still remembered his mother's warning to him:

"Do not forsake the children of God my son, never forsake the children of God."

Dad would lament this point during his 24year stay in Jeddah, even whilst continuing to show staunch support for the Arab Islamic cause.

Dad's realization that he had to pick sides

Dad realized that he had to pick sides in this Isaac/Ishmael tussle at a spiritual level, which was in contrast to his intransigence towards picking sides in the Political East/West "Cold

War" conflict during his reign as President of Uganda between 1971 and 1979.

I always thought Dad should have called the encounter with the beautiful female Mossad Agent, "The Spy who loved me". The enchantress later intimated a possible ruse, that she was a niece to General Moshe Dayan when Dad expressed admiration for the 6day war hero. Just before Dad left the land of Ramesis II, they both took a day off and went sightseeing at the mysterious Sphinx and Great Pyramids. One thing led to another and they found themselves in each other's arms. Conception was instant.

The beautiful female Mossad Agent left for New York and Dad headed back for the second confrontation with his Commander in Chief and Head of State of the 1st Republic of Uganda via Gulu Airbase, Jinja Airstrip and finally the old Entebbe Airport.

Ploys by the descendants of Isaac and Ishmael

The "mystical" events that unfolded in Egypt would be the beginning of systematic ploys by the feuding factions of descendants of Isaac and Ishmael to "use" Dad as a tool to advance their agendas in relation to their "fight to the death".

Dad's arrival from Abdel Nasser's funeral

Dad had sent word when he alighted in Gulu to all loyal officers to await information about his intended arrival. This had happened while the General Service Unit Operatives had "officially" rushed to Entebbe Airport awaiting his arrival on the official DC 4 (DAKOTA).

When the plane touched down at the Old Airport in Entebbe, the pilot was surprised by the heavily armed presence he received at the tarmac, only to tell them that he had left the Army Commander at the Gulu Airbase inspecting the facility. When Dad finally touched down at Entebbe his loyal officers led by one Captain Mustafa Adrisi met him at the tarmac. Then he was escorted with a heavy convoy to Kampala.

To cap it all, Dad then feigned Rheumatoid pains and was thus transported to the President's Office in a wheel chair. He was seeking the sympathy vote from his Commander in Chief when he came in as an invalid, to the astonishment of the Head of State according to one Abdul Latif who was part of the escorting team to the August House the very next day of Dad's arrival.

A standing ovation and continuing events

On October 7, 1970, Dad, Obote, Kenyatta and Nyerere attended an Inauguration Ceremony at Makerere University to make the university the University of East Africa. During that time, Obote became a Chancellor of the university.

At the Inauguration Ceremony, the students gave Dad a standing ovation after Obote had already arrested several politicians and begun investigating the death of Okoya while Dad was still in Cairo. Dad was supposed to be arrested on his return from Cairo but he returned and remained unharmed.

On October 9, 1970, Obote cancelled Uganda's 8th Independence Celebrations allegedly because of Gamal Abdel Nasser's death. It appeared however, that despite the trip to Egypt for Abdel Nasser's funeral, Dad was under "house arrest" and Obote was planning against him but he did not wish to risk antagonizing the army.

During October 1970, Steiner an Israeli mercenary allegedly helped train the Sudanese Anyanya in collaboration with Dad on Uganda soil. Steiner was arrested by the police in Uganda while trying to re-enter Uganda because of this allegation and he is quoted to have told the police that the Ugandan "Chief of Staff" helped him in his activities of training Anyanya from Uganda. However, it was really the late Brigadier Sulieman Hussien appointed by Obote as Army Commander while Dad was in Egypt for Abdel Nasser's funeral who helped Steiner in his activities relating to training the Anyanya.

It has been claimed that on December 19, 1970, Bar Lev the head of the Israeli Military Mission in Uganda was in Nairobi enroute to Israel. However, on December 20, 1970, Bar Lev returned to Kampala allegedly to plot the overthrow of Obote.

According to Dad, on January 11, 1971, Obote called him to his office and informed him of two things - the Report of the murder of Brigadier Okoya and his wife at Gulu and the Auditor-General's Report which alleged that Dad's Ministry of Defence had overspent £2,691,343.

On January 16, 1971, Dad held a Press Conference reiterating that there was a plan by Obote to have him (Dad) arrested by Obote's men.

On January 24, 1971, Obote flew to Singapore to attend the Commonwealth Conference while the head of the General Service Unit, Akena Adoko flew to London.

During the evening of January 24, 1971, Obote rang up the Officers' Mess at Jinja Barracks to instruct a trusted Aide believed to be Lieutenant Colonel Oyite-Ojok to arrest Dad and his immediate "underlings". However, a certain Kakwa Sergeant Major named Musa was said to have intercepted the message.

Meanwhile, Dad was wild duck shooting upcountry unaware of what was about to change his life and that of Uganda, until he was fortunately tipped off by a lady friend in the President's Office.

    Unbeknownst to Obote, the rift between him and Dad was to be the "perfect" setting for the fulfillment of the pronouncement made by Grandma Aisha Aate way back when Dad was an infant. A "friendship" gone terribly wrong would in effect be the force that would aid Dad's ascent to the "highest position in the land" of Uganda as pronounced and predicted by Grandma Aisha Aate after the Deadly "Paternity Test" Dad endured as an infant. The survival of the ordeal Dad endured on the slopes of the Kakwa Legendary Mountain Liru as an infant seemed to have become the norm as Dad survived one "liquidation plot" after another!

CHAPTER THREE

The day Dad overthrew Apollo Milton Obote

On January 25, 1971, Dad overthrew Apollo Milton Obote in a Military Coup, while Obote was in Singapore attending a Conference of Commonwealth Heads of State and Governments. Obote had eventually moved forward with his plan to get rid of Dad so he had relayed orders to his loyal Lan'gi officers to arrest Dad and his key Army supporters.

Over the years, Dad had bittersweet memories of the coup against Obote and it is to Mama Sauda Nnalongo that he owed his personal survival because she was the one who leaked word of the impending "plot" and plan to arrest Dad to him. Mama Sauda Nnalongo of the Babito of Bunyoro was one of Dad's women and at the time of the coup she was expecting twins that she delivered on April 4, 1971 - over two months after Dad's ascent to the "highest position in the land".

Some claim that it was Moses Ali who was then a Lieutenant at the Malire Station at Lubiri who saved Dad's life. However according to Dad, Moses Ali was a very reluctant participant who thought and acted like the teacher he was training to be in the 1960s. He said Mama Sauda Nnalongo was indeed the one who informed him of the impending doom and not Moses Ali. She got word of the telegram from Singapore and without hesitation secretly informed her man.

Unbeknownst to the "arresting team", Dad then instinctively swung into preemptive action. He decided to strike first and on January 25, 1971, while Obote was out of the country at a Commonwealth Conference of Heads of Government meeting in Singapore a coup was staged by the Army and Dad was declared President.

Dad relied on the Crack Team of Israeli and Sandhurst trained Junior Officers who had had their training in the Jewish Holy Land and Great Britain, to secure the key installations and garrisons across the country. On hindsight Dad didn't realize that the preemptive move would turn into a counter coup like some scene out of a Tom Cruise WWII German movie.

He quickly sought the loyalty of Pangarasio Onek in King George IV Garrison Jinja. Then he sought the loyalty of Erinayo Oryema who was the Head of Police at the time and had shown reluctance to go along with the plan to issue an arrest warrant against Dad when he attended the meeting that Obote convened before his departure to Singapore.

There are allegations that Dad's coup against Obote was backed by Israel and Britain both staunch supporters of Dad at the time of the coup but following is an outline of immediate

CHAPTER THREE

events surrounding the day of the Military Coup by Dad on January 25, 1971:

On January 25, 1971 at 2:00am, while most of the residents of Uganda were sleeping, Dad ascended to the "highest position in the land" of Uganda as pronounced and predicted by Grandma Aisha Aate after the Deadly "Paternity Test" he was subjected to as an infant.

The Kakwa son, Awon'go Idi Amin Dada, in a Dramatic Re-affirmation of "Rembi's Mystical Legacy" took over the Government of Uganda with the help of loyal troops.

Although the coup was largely bloodless, Dad's Biographer Judith Listowel claims that "two Canadian Roman Catholic priests, Father Jean Paul Demers and Father Gerald Perrault, were killed at Entebbe".

Things had come to a Head and Obote's counter move against Dad while attending that fateful Singapore Conference of Commonwealth Heads of State and Governments in 1971 were not Luo led but entirely Nubian led.

Army Chief of Staff Brigadier Sulieman Hussien, Air Force Chief of Staff Juma Musa and Buganda Police Chief Constable Sulieman Dusman were supposed to arrest and presumably liquidate Dad who was Commanding Officer right up to January 26, 1971.

Obote's "scheme" culminated in a century old affirmation of "Rembi's Mystical Legacy", when my father took over power from him. Indeed, Dad's mercurial rise during his military career from Private right through to Major General on the eve of his Coup D'etat is a testament to the Lan'ga na Da or "Stepping over the KAR rifle" ritual by my grandmother. That curiously "Yakanye-like" ritual was indeed a blessing in disguise.

Grandma was not present to witness the Coup D'etat that saw her son Awon'go Alemi ascend to the "highest position in the land" of Uganda as she pronounced after the Deadly "Paternity Test" Dad endured as an infant. She had died in August 1969, one year and a few months shy of the day she had looked forward to all her life. However, Dad had been content with the knowledge that Grandma had given him full blessings throughout his life and on her deathbed. He had been content with the knowledge that he had been by her side on the day of her demise and they had had the intimate conversation about the fact that she was proud of what he had achieved against all odds.

Dad had been very happy with the knowledge that Grandma had lived long enough to see him achieve the impossible and even partaken in the fruits of his incredible success. He was never going to forget Grandma's counsel regarding Lemi when she said, "In whatever you do make sure Lemi (justice, just cause, instinct, luck, absolute truth) is on your side then you will overcome every obstacle".

It is comforting to know that Dad later properly reconciled with Grandpa, after a cleansing ceremony facilitated by Elders from Grandma's Okapi-Bura/Lenya Clan of the Lugbara Tribe and Grandpa's Adibu Likamero Clan of the Kakwa tribe. Dad relented and after the ritual cleansing ceremony (which took place when Dad had achieved the impossible and had already become President of Uganda), Grandfather, the senior Amin Dada, was able to visit and actually stay with his son.

Dad placed his father at the Entebbe Lodge overlooking the lake front Entebbe Zoo which has now been transformed into a Wildlife Research Centre of sorts. Thus, until his death in the mid-1970s, Grandpa at least tasted his "Prodigal Son's" wealth. We used to be ushered towards the new wing at Entebbe Lodge to formally greet our Grandpa.

The rest is history as they say!

Many Ugandans welcomed the Military Coup by Dad on January 25, 1971 and vowed undying allegiance. Others took a more cautious "wait and see" approach. On the whole however, large crowds of Ugandans rejoiced deliriously. They demonstrated their support for Dad by flooding the streets of Kampala, "dancing" and "singing" to their hearts' content.

That memorable day, Dad became the Commander in Chief of Uganda, "The Pearl of Africa," the Head of State of the 2nd Republic of Uganda and he ruled Uganda from that January 25, 1971 until April 11, 1979 when he was overthrown and forced to live in exile with several of my family members, including me. We first lived in Libya and then in Saudi Arabia where Dad died on August 16, 2003.

"Detention Decree", foreign trips and a "plot"

On May 5, 1971, the Attorney General of Uganda announced an ill conceived "Detention Decree" enabling the Minister of Internal Affairs to detain any person who had "conducted or was conducting himself in a manner dangerous to peace and good order". The decree was supposed to last until March 1973 but it did not. Thus began Uganda's presumed slide into anarchy and dictatorship under Dad.

Meanwhile there was business as usual as Dad prepared to take trips to Britain and Israel. As this was happening, saboteurs began "hatching" and implementing insidious plans "crafted" to make Dad look like a whimsical murderer or someone who ordered brutal murders.

On July 1, 1971, Dad proceeded to meet the Queen in London. The British Elite continued "admiring him" as a "gentle giant" opposed to communism even though they would revoke their strong support for Dad one year later in 1972 when Dad stopped towing the puppet line of Subservience Protocol. Also in July 1971, Dad visited Israel and was received by Israel's Prime Minister Mrs. Golda Meir.

During his visit to England, Dad told the Queen about England being the only place he knew he could buy size 14 British shoes - probably his favourite "Church" shoes.

According to Dad, the Queen was beside herself and she was truly amused by the remark by her former subject who was part of the Guard Patrol when news came through in Kenya of the death of her father and her ascension to the British Throne. Dad was fond of reminding anyone of that little known fact.

A short-lived "honeymoon" with Israel

While on the trip to Israel, the Israelis presented Dad with an Executive Jet dubbed "Jet Commander." Israel also promised to sell Dad arms for up to $1 million while Britain agreed to supply Anti-Personnel Carriers (APCs) worth the same amount and to train fifty Ugandan officers.

Alas the honeymoon was short lived between the two nations of Israel and Uganda! Dad's erstwhile New Mentor Al-Faisal from Black Arabia (Saudi Arabia) was positioning himself on the distant horizon to replace the Israelis. His most loyal brother-in-arms Al-Qadhafi from the Magrib shores of Libya was also preparing to make his indelible mark on Dad's Psyche. This would come to the forefront after Dad and Al-Qadhafi's February 13-14, 1972 declaration of Indigenous Independence less than a year after the warm reception he received from Israel in July 1971.

The provocative question that King Faisal asked Dad during their secret meeting in Egypt in 1970 while attending Gamal Abdel Nasser's funeral would come home to roost in 1972 when Dad expelled the Israeli's from Uganda. As outlined in a previous section, that day, the King had asked Dad a typically provocative Muslim Question:

"You call yourself a Muslim Eid Al-Amin when you as Army Commander let your land be used for Zionist Hegemony over the Arab Muslim Nations?..."

The honeymoon with Britain would last a little longer but eventually wear off as well when Dad became "wayward", stopped "listening" and being a loyal servant and began "taunting" the British in the most unthinkable ways.

Dad had very friendly relations with both Israel and Britain considered friends of Uganda and Dad until the relationships failed. In fact in the early years of Dad's regime, the British Ambassador would sit in the cabinet meetings and the

Israeli Ambassador was a regular figure at Dad's cocktail parties. Furthermore, the British press loved Dad and praised him, often referring to him as the 'Gentle Giant'.

You will recall that in 1963, Dad was sent to Israel, despite being a Muslim. He had gone to Israel to take a Paratrooper Training course. While in Israel, Dad established strong relationships with members of the Israeli Elite. These relationships continued after Dad took over power from Apollo Milton Obote. The same relationships enabled Dad to supply arms to the Anyanya during the war in the Sudan between the predominantly Christian south and the predominantly Muslim North.

Prior to Dad's visit to Israel good news came his way around the American and French Independence days in 1971 when he had already achieved the impossible and was already the Head of State of the 2nd Republic of Uganda. That time, the Israeli Embassy sent him a "Private and Confidential" Post consisting of news about the birth to him of Jewish twin boys by the beautiful female Mossad Agent he had a secret meeting with in Egypt when he attended Gamal Abdel Nasser's funeral in 1970. According to Dad, his very close friend at the time, Colonel Baruch Balev sent him the "Private and Confidential" Post consisting the good news about our Jewish twin brothers.

You could almost see Dad's usual perplexed joy at knowing he had scored as he set eyes on pictures of the "Twin Bundles of Joy". "Twins!" he had thought to himself while reflecting that these were his second set of twins, for another woman who had also saved his life by warning him about another impending arrest this time immediately preceding the coup had also given him twins!

Dad could not help reflecting on the time in 1970 when he attended the funeral of Gamal Abdel Nasser in Egypt. He hadn't forgotten the beautiful female Mossad agent who asked to have a private meeting with him and intimated that she was sent on an urgent mission from New York to meet him and convey an urgent message from Colonel Balev. As outlined in an earlier section, the female Mossad agent had told Dad that his life was in danger and that Obote was rearranging the High Rank military structure so he should urgently return to Uganda but he was not to use the direct route to Entebbe. One thing had led to another and the results were the beautiful set of Jewish twins featured in the photograph he was now staring at in utter disbelief.

Dad's girlfriend Nnalongo Sauda who warned him about his impending arrest by Obote's High Command immediately preceding the Military Coup had given birth to a boy and a girl on April 4, 1971. Previous to that, Mama Kay had given birth to Ma'dira at the very hour Dad captured power on January 25, 1971. Now the mysterious lady – the beautiful female Mossad agent who also saved his life from Obote's "schemes" had placed the icing on the cake with Twins from the Judeo Holy Land!

In Uganda, the Baganda gave Dad the Honourary title Ssalongo, which is a title given to fathers of twins while the title Nnalongo is given to the mothers. Dad's title of Ssalongo would stick for the rest of the other sets of twins that followed over the next eventful years.

Friendships with King Faisal and Al-Qadhafi

In 1972, Dad established close friendships with King Faisal Bin Abdul Aziz Al-Saud of Saudi Arabia and Muamar Al-Qadhafi of Libya. The seeds for these friendships had been sown in 1970 when Dad attended the funeral of Gamal Abdel Nasser, the second President of Egypt.

The events that unfolded in Egypt "sealed" Dad's fate and they were the "prelude" to Dad's friendships with King Faisal Bin Abdul Aziz Al-Saud and Muamar Al-Qadhafi.

A break in the rock solid relationship with Israel

Prior to Dad's "shift in allegiances" from the descendants of Isaac to the descendants of Ishmael in their age-old "fight to the death", he had a rock solid relationship with Israel.

You will recall that the first two countries visited by Dad after he took over power from Apollo Milton Obote in 1971 were Britain and Israel. In July 1971, Dad visited Israel and he was received by Israel's Prime Minister Mrs. Golda Meir along with an admiring Colonel Balev and his colleague General Moshe Dayan.

Dad had very friendly relations with both Israel and Britain as has already been pointed out but the relations soured in 1972. During that year, Dad went on Pilgrimages to Makkah, Saudi Arabia. While on a trip to Makkah to join other Muslims around the world as they congregated at Makkah to visit the Kaaba – the most sacred site in Islam, he made a stopover in Libya and visited with Muamar Al-Qadhafi. Following the visit, Dad's relationship with Israel worsened very swiftly, as he took up with Muamar Al-Qadhafi and King Faisal Bin Abdul Aziz Al-Saud of Saudi Arabia and consolidated relationships with the two Muslim brothers. Dad would maintain these close relationships until his government was overthrown in April 1979 and beyond. While he was at the pinnacle of power in Uganda in the 1970s, he enjoyed support from Muamar Al-Qadhafi and King Faisal Bin Abdul Aziz Al-Saud and other Arab countries.

The close friendships between Dad and Muamar Al-Qadhafi and Dad and King Faisal Bin Abdul Aziz Al-Saud would ensure a safe passage

CHAPTER THREE 41

for our family first to Libya and then to Saudi Arabia where we led an opulent lifestyle after Dad was overthrown in 1979. However, the relationships would create a significant rift between Dad and Israel. The damage to the once warm and cordial relationship Dad and Israel shared would be irreparable. The relationship would disintegrate to a point of no return. While living in Saudi Arabia after his government was overthrown, Dad would also devote himself to Islam and be accorded the highest honour in Islam on the day of his demise on August 16, 2003.

According to information provided by Dad and other sources, following is a sketchy outline of what transpired in 1972 with respect to him crossing over to the "Arab" side of the age-old feud between the descendants of Ishmael and the descendants of Isaac and other events. The sketchy outline is for purposes of continuing to provide context to Dad's story and as a prelude to "fuller" information.

In February 1972, Dad went on a Pilgrimage to Makkah, which turned out to be a glorious occasion in Saudi Arabia following a mystic rainfall that Muslims in Saudi Arabia remember to this day. After the Pilgrimage to Makkah, Dad was called Al Hajj Idi Amin Dada, in compliance with the Islamic Rules of Pilgrimage to Makkah. Dad was also given a new Private Jet and the key to unlimited assistance "Wathiya" from the Saudi

Royal family. On this occasion, he was encouraged to discard the Executive Jet dubbed "Jet Commander" that had been given to him by Israel when he had visited Israel in 1971 and had been warmly received by Israel's Prime Minister Mrs. Golda Meir along with Colonel Balev and General Moshe Dayan and other Israeli Elite.

Unbeknown to Dad at the time, accepting the key to unlimited assistance "Wathiya" from the Saudi Royal Family and discarding the Executive Jet dubbed "Jet Commander" that had been given by Israel, was the beginning of being definitively caught between the warring descendants of Abraham's Children Ishmael and Isaac. The action by Dad would be in direct opposition to the gesture of warmth and endearing friendship that Israel extended to him over the years.

Drawing the lines and "dragging" Ugandans

The lines had been drawn and Dad had inadvertently "dragged" Ugandans into the age-old war between two perpetual enemies and warring factions determined to fight to the death to claim supremacy, legitimacy and land. In future years, Dad would continue to be caught in this vicious war and be way in over his head as the descendants of the two "sons of Abraham" continued to wrangle openly and involve "everyone" in their fight.

CHAPTER FOUR

Blood is thicker than water

Kakwa people know and abide by the adage "Blood is thicker than water". Traditionally, members of the Kakwa tribe know and don't dare violate that teaching even the ones who belong to the two religions of Islam and Christianity - the two dominant religions practiced by members of the Kakwa tribe. Kakwa Muslims who are unwavering supporters of the Arab people and Kakwa Christians who are unwavering supporters of the people of Israel have always lived together peacefully despite their "silent" support for the two warring factions.

They always know that Kakwa people don't dare fight because they belong to different religions. Dad was well aware of the teaching by Kakwa Temezi (Elders) to value blood relations over relations arising from religion and he even practiced it. However, I don't believe that he thought through the serious implications of his "jumping onto the band wagon" of the perpetual conflict between the descendants of Ishmael and Isaac. I don't believe he considered the seriousness of inadvertently being "dragged" into a war that would escalate into the event referred to as "The Entebbe Raid", earning him many enemies along the way. I outline this "Raid" in a subsequent section.

A reflection on the relationship with the Israelis

The Israelis acknowledge the good relationship they had with Dad before King Faisal Bin Abdul Aziz Al-Saud of Saudi Arabia and Muamar Al-Qadhafi of Libya came into the fray and I know Dad secretly lamented the split with the children of God as Grandma used to refer to the Israelis. Her point of reference was the teachings she received from being a practicing Catholic before she converted to Islam and immersed herself in its teachings as Grandpa and many members of my family did.

As outlined in previous sections, Grandma told Dad, "Do not forsake the children of God my son, never forsake the children of God" but alas a budding love relationship with the Israeli Nation was cut short at the roots.

King Faisal's gift to Dad of the Lear Jet

King Faisal Bin Abdul Aziz Al-Saud gave Dad the original Lear Jet "Gulf Stream II", free of charge. He intended it as a replacement for the Executive Jet dubbed "Jet Commander" that the Israelis gave Dad.

Dad never took the gift of the Lear Jet as his own, but preferred to refer to it as Ugandan State property. After his overthrow, the NRM Government pawned off the still functional Lear Jet and a GIII was bought in its stead.

During Dad's visit to Saudi Arabia for the Pilgrimage, he was also invested by King Faisal Bin Abdul Aziz Al-Saud with the highest Islamic Order – A Palm Tree Medal he would begin to wear to every occasion. The Palm Tree Medal was always pinned close to Dad's top button on all Military Dress he wore and discernible amongst a collage of other medals he collected from every Arab Islamic country he paid a visit to, following his visit to Saudi Arabia. Dad was honoured with accolades and faithfully honoured those who revered him by pinning their numerous accolades onto his broad chest, to the amusement of the Western Media. The Western media misinterpreted and conveyed this action by Dad as self aggrandizing behaviour and failed to note that the medals were to display the unwavering support he had for Arab people and Arab lands after severing ties with Israel.

A Diplomatic Relationship with Libya

On February 12, 1972, Roman Catholic Archbishop Mgr. Emmanuel Nsubuga, the Anglican Archbishop Dunstan Nsubuga and the Chief

Khadi of Uganda, Sheikh Abdularazak Matovu, flew with Dad to Libya.

On February 14, 1972 Dad and Muamar Al-Qadhafi signed and issued a Joint Communiqué in Tripoli relating to their unwavering support for the Arab People. This Joint Communiqué was actually Dad's declaration of Genuine Independence for Uganda, Africa and its Diasporas.

The Communiqué read:

"The two Heads of State undertake to conduct themselves according to the precepts of Islam. They assure their support to the Arab peoples in their struggle against Zionism and Imperialism for the liberation of confiscated lands and for the right of the Palestine people to return to their land and homes by all means".

Dad's audacious declaration in support of the Arab Peoples would permanently seal the "enmity" he now had with the People of Israel.

Following the Joint Communiqué signed and issued by Dad and Al-Qadhafi, Libya and Uganda decided to declare Diplomatic Relations and Al-Qadhafi accepted a formal invitation from Dad to visit Uganda at a date to be fixed later.

Al-Qadhafi assured Dad not to be intimidated by the Israelis and Zionists following the Joint Communiqué they issued, declaring support for the Arab peoples' rights and just struggle against Zionism and Imperialism. Because of the now strong relationship they shared, Al-Qadhafi in turn, appealed to Dad as an older, wiser man, to go and talk to the President of Tchad, Francois Tombalbaye. Al-Qadhafi was at war with Tombalbaye because of Tombalbaye's mistreatment of the Berber and Arab inhabitants of the northern area of Tchad. The Berber and Arab inhabitants of Tchad are Muslims who lived in the Tibesti Mountains and they called themselves the Tchad Liberation Front. Dad flew to Fort Lamy from Tripoli and after two days, he returned to Tripoli triumphantly with the news that Al-Qadhafi wanted.

In this euphoric atmosphere, Al-Qadhafi offered Dad financial aid on a much larger scale and on much better terms than Uganda had been receiving for some time. He became one of Dad's strongest allies and even promised Dad military assistance. Later that year 1972, Dad extensively toured the Middle East and returned with £40 million, which he received "with no strings attached" because he was "one of their own!"

On February 23, 1972, a ten-man Libyan delegation arrived in Uganda headed by Major El Maheidy.

On February 28, 1972, Uganda and Libya signed an agreement on economic and cultural cooperation.

In commemoration of their friendship, Dad changed the name King George IV, 4th Battalion of the Former Kings African Rifles Jinja Garrison to Al-Qadhafi Garrison. At the time of writing the

Introductory Edition of Idi Amin: Hero or Villain? His Son Jaffar Amin and Other People Speak, Al-Qadhafi had visited Uganda under President Yoweri Museveni and was charmed to know he had a garrison still bearing his name.

In February 1972, Dad summoned the Israeli Ambassador to Uganda and accused the Israelis of subversive activities. In future weeks, he would ask all Israeli citizens to leave Uganda.

The Addis Ababa Agreement for Peace

On March 17, 1972, the Addis Ababa Peace Agreement was signed between the rebel Anyanya movement of the Southern Sudan, led by General Joseph Lagu and the national Government of the Sudan headed by Jaffar Nimeiry. Henceforth, Obote transferred his troops from Owiny Kibul in the Sudan to a new and larger training camp at Handeni in Tanzania.

According to Dad and other sources, following the Addis Ababa Agreement that ended the First Sudanese War, frenzied activity occurred amongst Obote's humiliated Lan'go-Luo Sorbonne and Sandhurst trained Young Turks. They had to vacate their camp at Owiny Kibul in Southern Sudan where they had been supported by the Sudanese government to overthrow Dad while he "broke bread" with Israel.

Dad was in the process of severing ties with Israel and solidifying relationships with the Ummah (Community of Muslim Believers) instead so the two "warring" Muslims Dad and Jaffar Nimeiry saw it fit to end their hostilities. By 1972, Al-Qadhafi had brokered a Peace Deal between them, leading to a more cordial relationship between the two historical enemies. To "seal" the Peace Deal brokered by Al-Qadhafi that year, Dad and Jaffar Nimeiry opened and met over the Nimeiry Bridge on the Kaya River linking the Ora'ba and Kaya border towns of Uganda and Sudan respectively. This was a gesture of reconciliation and a sign of the cessation of hostilities between the two Muslim brothers.

Jaffar Nimeiry had never forgiven Dad for the direct support he provided to his fellow tribesmen in the Sudan during the southerners' insurgency led by Joseph Lagu from the Yei region of Sudan. The Northern Sudanese leader knew and dreaded Dad's ascension to the throne and his renowned long standing strong Israeli connections, which helped train and arm the Anyanya I insurgents in their long running War of Liberation from Arabinization and serfdom. Therefore he was willing and able to pragmatically support Obote's defeated troops after Dad took over power in the Military Coup. However, Al-Qadhafi showed concern about the possibility of two Muslim leaders confronting each other and like Faisal Bin Abdul Aziz Al-Saud of Saudi Arabia had done earlier, sought to lure Dad the newly installed Head of State of the 2nd Republic of Uganda to "permanently" cross over to the "Arab" side. Dad's potential had clearly been discernible by all who ever met him since his Kings African Rifles days in the 1940s and 1950s.

As the name denotes, the Addis Ababa Agreement was signed in the Ethiopian capital of Addis Ababa in the presence of Ethiopia's Emperor Haile Selassie.

The Addis Ababa Agreement, also referred to as the Addis Ababa Accord was signed to end the first Sudanese Civil War which occurred between 1955 and 1972 over a demand by insurgents in Southern Sudan for more regional autonomy. The first Sudanese War was also known as Anyanya I. The term "Anyanya" had been coined from the Amadi word Inyinya meaning poison. Amadi is a tribe in Southern Sudan.

According to reports, at the signing of the Peace Agreement in March 1972, Abel Alier signed the Agreement for the Government of the Sudan while General Joseph Lagu signed it on behalf of the Anyanya. Aggrey Jaden, a Pojulu by tribe was supposed to have been the one to sign the agreement on behalf of the Anyanya but being less educated than Lagu and not being a military graduate, Jaden thought it wise for Lagu to sign the agreement on behalf of the Anyanya instead.

CHAPTER FOUR

The Addis Ababa Agreement lasted from 1972 to 1983 when it broke down resulting in the civil war between John Garang's Sudan People's Liberation Army (SPLA) and the Government of the Sudan. The relative peace that had followed the signing of the Agreement in March 1972 was disrupted when the former president of Sudan Jaffar Nimeiry imposed Shari'a throughout the country including the very Southern Sudan that had fought for Autonomy but settled for semi Autonomy with the signing of the Agreement.

Shari'a is the body of Islamic religious law and legal framework within which the public and private aspects of life are regulated for those living in a legal system based on Islamic Principles of Jurisprudence. Shari'a deals with many aspects of day-to-day life, including politics, economics, banking, business, contracts, family, sexuality, hygiene and social issues.

17 years of bloodbath had come to an end finally - or so it was thought in March 1972 when a somewhat uneasy agreement was signed between the rebel Anyanya movement of the Southern Sudan and the national Government of the Sudan but war would erupt again in 1983.

The Addis Ababa Agreement that ended Anyanya I did not completely address the reasons that had caused this first war in the first place. As a result, war erupted again between Northern

Sudan and Southern Sudan, a mere decade after the signing of the Agreement.

Eye witnesses reported watching and participating in mass demonstrations in Juba, the capital city of Southern Sudan leading to the Second Sudanese Civil War, with crowds repeatedly chanting "Kokora" (which means division in the "Bari languages") and "Nimeiry, we want separation" in Arabic. The "Bari languages" include the Kuku, Bari, Kakwa and Pojulu languages among others.

The Second Sudanese Civil War is commonly referred to as Anyanya II and it lasted from 1983 to 2005. The two conflicts that occurred in the Sudan between 1955 and 2005 are sometimes considered one conflict with an eleven-year cease-fire and hiatus separating the two wars.

According to Dad, following the signing of the Addis Ababa Agreement in 1972, he used his 20,000 strong tribes-mates from the Sudan who could not go back to the Sudan or chose to stay in Uganda, to expand his army. This arrangement had also been part of an agreement between himself and Jaffar Nimeiry as Muslim brothers. Instead of letting the former Anyanya I soldiers "roam about with no purpose" after the end of the First Sudanese war, Dad integrated many of them into the Uganda Army and actually sent a substantial number for extensive military courses abroad. This decision boosted his army to a resounding 45,000 strong by the time his government was overthrown in 1979.

Meanwhile Dad's exiled former mentor Dr. Apollo Milton Obote was forced to transfer his loyal troops from Southern Sudan to the northern region of Tanzania following the uneasy Peace Agreement between President Jaffar Nimeiry and General Joseph Lagu and the agreement between Dad and Jaffar Nimeiry as Muslim brothers.

Dad's 180-degree turn against Israel

Dad's change in allegiances from the Israelis to the Arabs was to precipitate a melt-down of the Israeli-Uganda special relationship starting with the immediate and "shocking" expulsion of all Israeli firms and citizens from Uganda by Dad. The melt- down would culminate in the 1976 Israeli Hostage saga dubbed "The Entebbe Raid" which is outlined in a subsequent section.

The opportunity for Dad to "permanently" cross over to the "Arab" side arose when Dad made an unexpected extended visit to Israel in July 1971 to meet Golda Meir of Israel and onwards to England to meet Queen Elizabeth II with a special request for heavy armory.

Alas! Dad's requests for armaments were rejected by supposed allies Israel and Great Britain. Feeling dejected, he made a pre-arranged but undisclosed detour to Cairo where he met a high profile amalgamation of the Arab League's Leadership. They had picked up concern laid out in The Times Magazine around a question relating to the enormous build up of activity at Nakasongola Airbase in Uganda.

The combined echelon of the Arab League Leadership intimated King Faisal Bin Abdul Aziz Al-Saud's previous 1970 pronouncement and grave concern when he quizzed:

"You call yourself a Muslim Eid Al-Amin when you as Army Commander let your land be used for Zionist Hegemony over the Arab Muslim Nations in Africa and the Middle East? Have you ever sat down and asked yourself why Uganda would need a sixteen capacity simultaneous takeoff runway, for F4 Phantom Jets on your land, if not but to be a southern hemisphere rear base to enable the illegitimate Jewish state to attack Arab Muslim countries from the southern Hemisphere? Ask yourself sincerely......"

During Dad's undisclosed detour to Cairo, he was able to meet the following Arab leaders:

Anwar Al-Sadat of Egypt

Hafez Al-Assad of Syria

Muamar Al-Qadhafi of Libya

Deep down, Dad felt an overwhelming sense of betrayal from those he felt intimately loyal to, namely Britain and the Jewish Nation. So, despite his mother's plea to "never forsake the children of God", at this critical juncture Dad was

CHAPTER FOUR

all ears to the illustrious group of Arab League Heads of State. He was convinced that they would honour his request for armaments after his supposed allies Israel and Great Britain rejected the request. That time, Dad was able to make an unscheduled detour to Libya which culminated in the Joint Communiqué and declaration between the Peoples' Great Jamahiriyah of Libya and the 2nd Republic of Uganda on February 13 -14, 1972.

As a now more committed "African Muslim", Dad miraculously managed to quell and foster an "uneasy truce and peace agreement" between Libya and the Republic of Tchad, to the amazement of his Host Al-Qadhafi. Pumped up with revolutionary fervor, Dad then made his return journey to Uganda. From that time onwards, the world was in for an Apple Cart Suplex upset from the least expected of Wrestling Ring Corner since they felt they had installed "Big Daddy" on the throne. They expected nothing short of dogged loyalty and Subservience Protocol from the Kakwa native whom they thought they knew so well!

As a bonus for crossing over to the Ummah (Community of Muslim Believers) and "Arab" side, Dad was given his second most favourite mode of transport between 1972 and 1979 by Saudi Arabia – the original Lear Jet "Gulf Stream II". It was second only to his famous SM Citroen

Maserati, a metallic Green Mercedes Benz 300 SE Coupe, which was given by Al-Qadhafi.

Having completely crossed over to the "Arab" side of the age-old tussle between the descendants of Ishmael the Arabs and the descendants of Isaac the Israelis, Dad took a very hostile stance towards the Israelis. He severed his relationship with Israel after taking up with the Ummah (Community of Muslim Believers) and "vowing" to be a devout Muslim from then onwards:

On March 23, 1972, Israel firmly denied interference in Uganda's Internal Affairs following an accusation by Dad. However, despite the denial, Dad called for all Israel military instructors to leave on the grounds of "subversive activities."

On March 25, 1972, Dad cancelled all arms deals with Israel and stopped work on civilian construction contracted by Israeli companies, including the Arua Airport.

On March 27, 1972, Dad ordered all Israeli firms to leave Uganda.

On March 30, 1972, Dad ordered the Israeli Embassy to be closed.

On March 31, 1972, Israel published the true number of her citizens working in Uganda (149 with their wives and children, 470 in total).

CHAPTER FIVE

The time the last Israelis left Uganda

On April 8, 1972, the last Israelis left Uganda. According to Dad, the Israelis claimed that Uganda owed them £9 million for airports, training equipment and economic losses.

The rest of April and May 1972 were relatively quiet months in Uganda. However, on April 15, 1972, Uganda and Britain signed an agreement on military training.

On April 19, 1972, Dad announced that Libya agreed to (a) Build two hospitals in Uganda (b) Train Ugandan pilots and technicians and (c) Provide instructors for the Uganda Armed Forces.

On April 28, 1972, a full training team from Britain led by Colonel Rogers arrived in Uganda.

In May 1972, a Saudi delegation headed by the Director-General of the Islamic World Union arrived in Kampala where a Supreme Muslim Council was to be set up in Uganda.

At the end of May 1972, an Iraqi delegation visited Uganda and Dad called for the establishment of a regional military alliance for Arab and African States because "all the seas around the African continent belonged to African or Arab nations", he asserted in his distinctive bombastic style. It was around this time in 1972 that Dad started to passionately embrace the African cause as well. He had despised colonialism but he hadn't been as vocal and public about it until this time in 1972. So, in June 1972, he made it public that he was going to the Organization of African Unity (OAU) Conference in Rabat, Morocco.

The OAU was predecessor to the African Union (AU) and its aims included promoting the unity and solidarity of African states, acting as a collective voice for the African continent and eradicating all forms of colonialism. Both the OAU and the AU will be explored in more detail in subsequent parts of the series, Idi Amin: Hero or Villain? His Son Jaffar Amin and Other People Speak. However, on June 10, 1972, Dad left for Rabat and stopped in Tripoli to visit with his staunch supporter Muamar Al-Qadhafi. He left Charles Oboth Ofumbi as Acting Vice President in his absence.

On June 18, 1972, Dad was back from the Organization of African Unity (OAU) Conference in Rabat, Morocco.

Rumours of a coup and a return from a Tour

Meanwhile, it was rumoured that individuals from the Lugbara tribe were "planning" to overthrow Dad's regime.

On June 23, 1972, Dad was back in Kampala from an Arab Tour and he came home with £40 million "with no strings attached" because he was a Muslim brother.

On June 29, 1972, Dad left for Egypt and from there proceeded to Algeria, Tunisia, Syria, Jordan, Saudi Arabia and the Sudan to visit with Arab and Muslim Heads of State.

On July 1, 1972, Colonel Roger's British Training Team consisting of 4 Company Commanders and 12 NCOS (Non Commissioned Officers) began a military course for the Uganda Army. Lieutenant Colonel Francis Nyangweso, the Army Commander opened the course in Jinja, which ended on August 25, 1972.

On July 2, 1972, Dad saw Al-Qadhafi in Tripoli as he flew from Bonn, West Germany.

On July 6, 1972, a Palestine Liberation Organization (PLO) delegation visited Uganda and the delegation was entertained in the vacated Israeli Embassy.

At the end of July 1972, Dad announced that Al-Qadhafi had granted Uganda £3.4 million and pledged Libya to buy Uganda coffee and cotton to the tune of £11.6 million a year.

Friendships with African leaders and an agenda

Dad had friendly relationships with many African leaders including Jean-Bédel Bokassa of the Central African Republic and Siad Barre of Somalia. As he strengthened friendships with many African Heads of State, he continued to forge forward with his agenda for the African cause alongside his agenda for the Arab cause. However, his relatively consistent - perhaps the most consistent aspect of his policies as President of Uganda was his most controversial anti-Israeli/Anti Zionist orientation and strong Pro-Palestinian/Pro-Arab stance since meeting with Malik Faisal Bin Abdul Aziz Al-Saud of Saudi Arabia in the 1970s. This fateful act continued to pay off even after his turbulent overthrow in April 1979. Dad enjoyed the privilege of being a lifetime guest of the Royal Family's hospitality and generosity partly in return for his dedicated pro-Arabism.

The loyal Kings African Rifles soldier whose father was converted to Islam by Sultan Ali Kenyi at the turn of the 20th century now resides in the heartland of Sunni Islam, the ancestral home of the Messenger of Allah, the original Dar-El-Islam among fellow Believers. Dad was supremely aware, despite several disclaimers as to his ability to effectively rule Uganda under an embargo for eight years! Since our Kakwa tribe was a tiny fraction of approximately 150,000 strong in a population of over 14 million at the time, it did therefore make political sense to Dad to cultivate additional constituencies including his very own Ummah (Community of Muslim Believers).

CHAPTER FIVE 61

As I stated in a previous section, before Grandpa was converted to Islam, he was a practicing Roman Catholic. His first name was Andrea right up to and during the first decade of the 20th Century from 1900 to 1910. His full name at the time was Andrea Dada son of Nyabira, who in turn was the son of Dada of the Adibu Likamero Kakwa clan. Grandpa was converted to Islam by a fellow Kakwa with the title Sultan Ali Kenyi of the Drimu Kakwa clan of Ko'buko (Ko'boko) - perhaps the most notorious, influential, and towering Ugandan Kakwa Chief in the first half of the 20th century. One of four Sultans appointed by the Colonial Administration, Sultan Ali Kenyi who was also a Hereditary Chief was highly respected by colonial administrators and both revered and feared by his subjects the Kakwa. He had no tolerance for dissent and administered lashings that left dissidents squirming in pain for weeks - even months. During his tenure as Sultan and Chief of the Kakwa, Ali Kenyi cultivated a friendship with Major C.H. Stingard who had a particular fondness for Kenyi's Kakwa tribe.

Dad's stance to cultivate additional constituencies including his very own Ummah because our Kakwa tribe was a tiny fraction of approximately 150,000 strong in a population of over 14 million at the time was directly parallel to the Petrol Dollar Era in the 1970s. He was precisely in power during the heyday of OPEC (Organisation of Petroleum Exporting Countries) during the period 1971 to 1979 and as an organisation OPEC is overwhelmingly Muslim in composition. The Aid distribution behavior of OPEC or OAPEC (Organisation of Arab Petroleum Exporting Countries) has tended to be to help firstly fellow Arabs and secondly fellow Muslims and thirdly fellow so-called third world countries, provided there is some evidence of support and sympathy for the Arab cause. Under Dad and despite the fact that Muslims remain a minority in Uganda, Uganda benefited considerably from OPEC sources. This was because Dad was a Muslim Head of State who was also staunchly Pro-Palestinian as well as a dedicated and consistent friend of Arabs - once he had made the decision to break ties with the Israelis in 1972.

Dad had once trained as a paratrooper in Israel and continued to wear Israeli Wings to his last days at the helm of power but the relationship with Israel had disintegrated beyond repair.

I liken Dads' split with the Israelites to Muhammad Ali's schism with Malik Al-Shabbaz considering the extremely close relationship they had.

One time, Dad related to me how he survived a helicopter crash with an Israeli pilot and they instinctively decided to become "blood brothers", by severing themselves and mingling each other's blood in remembrance of their ordeal.

CHAPTER FIVE

As outlined in previous sections, another close blood-tie Dad had in Israel was a claim he had of having fathered twins with a female Mossad agent who fortunately fell for him in Cairo during the time he attended the funeral of Gamal Abdel Nasser in Egypt in 1970.

I fondly call my two unknown siblings Izrael Adule and Israel Dombu and their mother apparently has a lineage to Moshe Dayan who was a General when Dad visited Israel in 1971. Israel and Dad had very strong relationships at the time.

While we lived in exile in Saudi Arabia, I often wondered and actually asked Dad if he would like to meet up with these children but he bluntly told me off and said that these kids were nothing more than enemies as far as he was concerned. I was taken aback, much in the same way I felt when the famous Boxer Muhammad Ali commented that anyone who crossed Elijah Muhammad, the Supreme Minister of the United States based "Nation of Islam" from 1934 until his death in 1975 deserved what they got more or less. At the time I asked Dad about our Jewish siblings, I still felt the distinct nostalgic longing for the good old days.

Despite the outward support for the Arab people and the Ummah (Community of Muslim Believers), it was obvious that Dad was in conflict within himself about his relationship with Israel. The irony of it all was that as Dad continued to openly support the Ummah, he never ever severed relationships with members of our family who were Christians. He was consistent in adhering to the teaching by Kakwa Temezi (Elders) to value blood relations over relations arising from religion and he even practiced it. That is the reason why he used to label the false claims about him persecuting Christians in Uganda during his rule as pure "Parapaganda" (Propaganda). It was part of the ongoing slander and conspiracy meant to shed Dad in a terrible light and bring him down. Like all the false allegations relating to Dad, the false allegations about Dad persecuting Christians would be blindly accepted as truth without anyone ever investigating how close and intimate Dad's relationships were with Christian family members, Christian associates, other Ugandans who were Christians and other Christians elsewhere.

As a matter of fact, in 1972, Dad in his usual bombastic utterances wanted two of his sons to become Roman Catholic Priests and they were already in Roman Catholic Seminary. Come to think of it by this time, I together with the following had been relocated from Al-Qadhafi Garrison in Jinja and sent in the company of our Foster Parent Sergeant John Katabarwa to live with Grandpa Sosteni:

1. My sister Sofia Sukeji

2. My younger brother Khamis Machomingi and

3. Our cousin Joseph (Yusuf) Akisu

Until these new living arrangements, we had resided with our Foster Parents Sergeant John Katabarwa and his wife Joyce. At the time we moved in with Grandpa Sosteni, he was stationed at the Simba Battalion in Mbarara. While residing at Grandpa Sosteni's, we attended Preschool at a Catholic Seminary School near Ntare Senior Secondary School and spent most times watching Celluloid Films. If Dad hated and persecuted Christians as it has been falsely alleged, he would never have sent us to Christian Mission Schools more so daring the likes of Al-Amin Mazrui to convert two of his biological children Tshombe (me) and Machomingi to Christianity.

Support for the Ummah and consolidating Islam

In 1972, Dad continued his agenda to demonstrate his support for the Ummah (Community of Muslim Believers) and to promote Islam in Uganda. That year, he visited the late Badr Kakungulu at his Kibuli Mosque with a proposal to build a large Mosque which Muslims from all over Uganda could call their own. They stood on the Kibuli hillside looking at the expanse of Kampala and its famous 7 hills. The new Head of State of Uganda (Dad) then commented to his Royal

Highness, "This looks like the best place for the Headquarters of the Muslim Supreme Council" he intimated.

However taken aback by the abrupt visit from Dad and feeling threatened, his Royal Highness bravely answered "Etaka te Tundilwa" ("Land is never sold"). Dad shrugged his shoulders and said, "Okay". Then he strode to his awaiting SM Citreon Maserati and took off to his Official Parliament Presidential Office at Parliament Building. According to Dad, the next time he and the late Badr Kakungulu would collide would be during the infamous 1976 Nsambia grenade attack on his life that killed his driver Musa after the Police Pass Out of the new Recruits.

That time, Dad requested his Permanent Secretary to find out through the Town Clerk and the Land Board if there was any land in the city that was available for his grand designs. Luckily the response was positive from the Permanent Secretary. Apparently the Lease on Fort Lugard had expired and was ready for the taking. Overjoyed, Dad called up his chum Qassim Ramadhan, nicknamed "No Parking". Qassim acquired this nickname because he was the smallest Rugby Player who played as a Forward during their Rugby Playing days. He was a little rum and used to wade into the others at the Jinja Rugby Grounds. This was the same place Dad took them to play after the 1964 mutiny he helped stop. He

CHAPTER FIVE

got the nickname for his ferocious Defense and bringing down attacking wingers from the other teams. Qassim Ramadhan ("No Parking") was then Governor of southwestern Uganda.

Dad and Qassim Ramadhan then drove up to Kapere's deserted House on the hill. Lord Lugard was called Kapere by the Baganda for he favoured the checkered short sleeved shirts.

High up on Old Kampala Hill overlooking the Business District Centre, Dad asked "No Parking" in Kinubi (the language of the de-tribalised community referred to as the Nubi (Nubians)) - looking towards Namirembe Hill, "De be ta munu?" ("Whose house is that?") "No Parking" answered, "Church of Uganda". Dad arched his head round over to Rubaga and made the same inquiry. "Catholic Church", responded his most trusted Aide.

Dad then pointed across the expanse of the Buganda Road Bus Park over to the Hindu Temple, which was built brick by brick without using steel or concrete right up to the height of three storeys. Then down towards the Ismailia Mosque, occupied by the newly installed Muslim Supreme Council right below where they stood and lamented:

"All the other faiths have a national place where they gather, yet we Muslims only have places of worship that belong to individuals".

The above happened because Buganda is the land of Overloads and Serfs since the "1900 Agreement" - the very few haves and the majority serfs who are the have nots - Kibuli, Wandegeya even Speedika in Ntinda.

"Why can't we have a place where Muslims from Karamoja, Arua, Bushenyi, Kabale or even Mbale and Tororo can call their own? Insha Allah this will be the spot right here where we plant the Liwa (Banner) of Islam. We will plant the Banner proclaiming La Illah Illah Allah Muhammad Rasul Allah right here where the British planted the Union Jack," Dad intimated with profound determination glinting in his eyes. He ensured a 99-year Lease was processed.

As if to give a very public nod of approval for Dad's passion to be a champion of Islam, a most memorable and rare event took place when Malik Faisal Bin Abdul Aziz Al-Saud of Saudi Arabia made a show of support to Dad by visiting Uganda in the early seventies. While on this trip, Dad gave the King of Saudi Arabia a tour of the Magnificent Masjid Noor in Bombo. He also organized an impromptu Picnic at a Picnic site near the Mabira Forest on the way to Jinja.

You will recall that this Magnificent Masjid was built by the de-tribalised community referred to as the Nubi (Nubians) that emerged from 19th century political upheavals in Africa that were linked to the colonization of Sub-Saharan Africa.

During the 19th century, the original mercenary community that was predominantly Muslim was transferred to the newly built Army Headquarters Barracks in Bombo in present day Luwero District in the Great Kingdom of Buganda.

As introduced in previous sections and discussed more fully in subsequent parts of the series, Idi Amin: Hero or Villain? His Son Jaffar Amin and Other People Speak, the Vanguard Mercenary Troops of the New Protectorate Army under the Command of Colonel Colville, settled in Bombo under a donation from His Majesty Kabaka (King) Daudi Chwa of the Great Kingdom of Buganda. They built the Magnificent Masjid Noor in Bombo in the early 1900s. The structure holds so much majesty and historical significance that it impresses everyone who has the privilege of entering it.

Because of our Islamic roots, many members of my family became amalgamated with the de-tribalised community referred to as the Nubi (Nubians) and referred to themselves as such. In the early years of his youth, Dad attended Garaya (School of Qur'anic Studies/Readings) at this location so he was well acquainted with the structure.

During his visit to Uganda, Dad showed King Faisal Bin Abdul Aziz Al-Saud around the Magnificent Mosque and the Late King was mesmerized and his confidence strengthened when he beheld this ancient structure in the most unexpected of places. The King marveled at the Magnificent Masjid Noor during his visit to Uganda in 1972 and never stopped talking about it.

When Dad gave the late King a personal tour of the ancient structure in 1972, he also went on to introduce his former Madrasah classmates. Amongst these classmates, the most famous one was the adept Sheikh Abdul Qadr Aliga. Of course the other one was Dad himself. Both Sheikh Abdul Qadr Aliga and Dad were trained in the esoteric practices at this Khanqah where they won honors in their youth in Alim Al Qur-an (the Quranic Scholar), in the 1930s and 1940s under the guardianship of the late Sheikh Al-Rajab.

Dad remarked that the most touching moment during King Faisal Bin Abdul Aziz Al-Saud's visit was when he arranged an impromptu picnic for the King en-route to Jinja. Dad surprised him by setting up a picnic at a site located in the middle of the now endangered Mabira Rain Forest on the right hand side shoulder of the forest as you head to Jinja from Kampala.

Actually to this day, if one makes an effort, you can see this particular picnic site on your right shoulder as you proceed to Jinja. The site has concrete park benches strewn around the blissful locale which always reminds me of scenes from "Snow White and the Seven Dwarfs" when she had managed to evade her step-mother with gentle cascades of sun rays with tiny gold dust particles lighting up the forest floor.

Malik Faisal Bin Abdul Aziz Al-Saud was so taken in by the wonderful surroundings and the scene so overwhelmed him that he remarked to his host:

"This surely must be how heaven must look like Allaaah!"

Dad was ecstatic and truly touched by the King's remarks and the praise showered on the beauty of his homeland and country Uganda by his illustrious and most honourable guest. That same year, he had made two pilgrimages to Mecca and met King Faisal Bin Abdul Aziz Al Saud and other leaders of several Muslim countries who had also come to Mecca. During the King's visit, he praised Dad's measures against Israel and promised Dad assistance in strengthening Islam in Uganda.

The late King Faisal Bin Abdul Aziz Al-Saud never forgot Dad's unwavering support for the Arab People, along with his visits to the Kingdom of Saudi Arabia and the impromptu picnic he set for his VIP guest when he visited Uganda in 1972.

Years later while reminiscing about his past at our Al Safa residence in Saudi Arabia, Dad recalled the picnic at Mabira Rain Forest while lamenting the loss of what he claimed to have had

- a beautiful voice! Dad claimed that he lost his beautiful voice following a brutal Illegal Hook by an unscrupulous Zania (South African) Boer Frontlines Man in a Rugby Match in the 1950s.

He was then the only Indigenous Rugby player allowed to use the facility at the Jinja Rugby Club at the height of colonial segregation following the incident relating to him challenging the racism and segregation that was rampant in colonial and "segregated" Uganda at the Officers' Mess in 1959.

As I recounted in a previous section, Dad had dared to march into the "Whites Only" Officers' Mess at 1st Battalion Jinja after being promoted to the Honourary Rank of Affende - the highest rank awarded to Black African members of the Kings African Rifles at the time. He got tired of moving with a rank that did not hold water and moved up to the "Whites Only" Officers' Mess instead of going to the Sergeants' Mess and ordered a drink. When the White Bartender told Dad off and "barked" for him to go to the Sergeants' Mess, Dad beat up the Bartender, forced a change in the segregative rule and got invited to join the exclusive "Whites Only" Jinja Rugby Club because he was "one of their own".

Dad claimed that after the brutal illegal hook by the unscrupulous Zania Boer Frontlines Man in the Rugby Match, which he considered as a deliberate attempt by the Boer Frontlines Man to

CHAPTER FIVE

put him out and in his place as a Kaffir, he never again regained that beautiful voice - hmmmm!

Kaffir was a word used by bigoted South African Whites during the time South Africa practiced the reprehensible Apartheid System of segregation to refer to Black Africans.

CHAPTER SIX

Dad's 1973 "Dream Speech" at the OAU

In May 1973, Dad attended and addressed the Organization of African Unity (OAU) Summit in Addis Ababa, Ethiopia.

Established in 1963 by 37 "Independent" African nations, the OAU was formed to promote unity and development, defend the sovereignty and territorial integrity of members, eradicate all forms of colonialism, promote international cooperation and coordinate members' economic, diplomatic, educational, health, welfare, scientific and defense policies. At the time of its formation, the OAU was synonymous with Pan-Africanism, a term generally used for African movements whose aims include unifying "Africans" and eliminating colonialism and white supremacy from the African continent. Among several things, the OAU mediated internal and external disputes involving Member States and it played a significant role in ending Apartheid in South Africa, which became the 53rd OAU Member State in 1994.

The African Union (AU), established in 2002 by the OAU states is a successor to the OAU. The AU has been commissioned with more powers to promote African economic, social, and political integration and a stronger commitment to democratic principles. It also aims to promote unity and solidarity among African states, act as a catalyst for economic development and promote international cooperation, among other things. The OAU had similar goals to the AU but the AU is more economic in nature and it has a stronger mandate to intervene in conflicts occurring on the African continent between Member States, as one of its objectives is the promotion of peace, security and stability in Africa.

The 53 African states that were members of the OAU are also members of the African Union, which includes a Pan-African Parliament, inaugurated in 2004. The Pan-African Parliament also known as the African Parliament is the legislative body of the African Union. After its inauguration in 2004, the Pan-African Parliament agreed to create a peacekeeping force, which has since been actively involved in peacekeeping efforts in various parts of Africa.

The Organization of African Unity, Pan-Africanism and the African Union will all be explored in more detail in subsequent parts of the series, Idi Amin: Hero or Villain? His Son Jaffar Amin and Other People Speak, along with how they evolved and what the future holds for Africa and its Diaspora's in relation to them. In particular, the involvement of descendants of Africans "stolen" from Africa during the "African Slave Trade" in the Emancipation of Africa will be given special consideration, as the success of Africa and its Diasporas is intimately connected to the Emancipation of All "African Peoples" around the world! However, suffice it to state here that Dad really embraced the OAU's aims relating to promoting the unity and solidarity of African states, acting as a collective voice for the African continent and eradicating all forms of colonialism and many other aims. He wanted Africa and its Diasporas liberated from all the "chains of oppression" but his saboteurs and detractors would not let him implement the noble vision he had!

Throughout his rule, Dad faced intense and unprecedented sabotage that started immediately after he took over power from Apollo Milton Obote in January 1971. As outlined in a previous section, Dad used to lament that he only ruled Uganda for one day because Ugandan exiles started subversive activities the very second day of his rule. According to him, these subversive activities included Ugandan exiles operating within Uganda, kidnapping and murdering prominent Ugandans and in some cases even foreigners, so that it looked like his operatives were committing the brutal murders.

As if the sabotage by Ugandan exiles wasn't enough, a powerful media soon began "lynching" Dad when he couldn't be "controlled". They did it the same way African slaves who dared to run away, defy or challenge "rules" imposed on them during the "African Slave Trade" were lynched. However, Dad's "lynching" was done by making unsubstantiated allegations against him and putting them in print or film for "everyone" to blindly accept as truth. The form of "lynching" was intended for "anything" and "everything" written, said and depicted about Dad to be the "gospel truth". Dad's saboteurs, detractors and a powerful media thus succeeded in undermining and stopping his efforts to liberate "oppressed groups" until he fell without accomplishing the noble vision he had.

During his address to the OAU Summit in Addis Ababa in 1973, Dad articulated his dream for Africa while listing some of Africa's problems and how they might be solved. He took a Pan Africanist stance and argued for many of the solutions to Africa's problems. The solutions Dad proposed and implemented for Africa's problems during his rule will be discussed in subsequent parts of the series, Idi Amin: Hero or Villain? His Son Jaffar Amin and Other People Speak.

However an article by Bamuturaki Musinguzi titled "Amin's dream for Africa" which includes information about what Dad said during his address to the Organization of African Unity in Addis Ababa, Ethiopia in May 1973 provides insight into Dad's passion for the liberation of Africa. The article was published in 2006 and it

CHAPTER SIX

conveys many of Dad's thoughts and actions relating to his vision for Africa.

At the 1973 OAU Summit in Addis Ababa, Ethiopia, Dad spoke in his usual bombastic manner. He wanted true Independence for "African People" everywhere and in subsequent "conversations" and speeches, he would assert in his usual bombastic style:

"Let me tell you!" "Africa is for Africans."

"We want true Independence for all Peoples of Africa".

"Africa is Strong!" "Africa is Independent and Self-sufficient."

"We need to understand the need to come together!"

Every time issues relating to the Emancipation of Africa and its Diasporas came up, Dad became as passionate, animated and bombastic as he did at the 1973 OAU Summit in Addis Ababa, Ethiopia. The thoughts conveyed by him in his address to the Organization of African Unity in May 1973 speak for themselves!

In subsequent parts of the series, Idi Amin: Hero or Villain? His Son Jaffar Amin and Other People Speak, there will be opportunities to discuss (1) The solutions "presented" by Dad at the OAU Summit in Addis Ababa, Ethiopia in May 1973 and thereafter, for the liberation of Africa, (2) Assertions he made in his address to the OAU Summit in Addis Ababa, Ethiopia in May

1973, (3) Excerpts from the book referred to by Bamuturaki Musinguzi in his article titled "Amin's dream for Africa," (4) Assertions he made about Africa in subsequent "conversations" and speeches, (5) Actions he took as Head of State of Uganda to realize the solutions he envisioned and presented for Africa's problems, along with the consequences of his "audacity" to "publicly" push for and pursue those solutions and (6) Any other issues relating to his legacy.

A champion for causes

In 1973, Dad continued demonstrating his unwavering support for Arab people and the Ummah (Community of Muslim Believers). Sometime that year, he gave a Press Conference in Damascus, Syria and voiced that unwavering support. The Arab and Muslim cause was one he had fully embraced by the year 1973.

As Dad publicly championed the cause of the Arab people and the Ummah, he also publicly championed the cause of Africa and its Diasporas. He pursued his agenda for the Emancipation of Uganda and the rest of Africa and its Diasporas with a passion and made many decisions consistent with what he eloquently articulated when he attended and addressed the Organization of African Unity (OAU) Summit in Addis Ababa, Ethiopia in May 1973.

After Dad "picked up" and fully embraced Pan-Africanism and the "African" cause, he had a very conflicted relationship with Britain, Uganda's former "Colonial Master". That conflict manifested itself as a series of "very public" "bad behaviours" by Dad towards Britain and its citizens while he continued to "praise" them in private and love all things British.

Dad's very first "very public" "bad behavior" directed at Britain and its citizens was the expulsion from Uganda in 1972 of Asians who either held British Passports or were entitled to British Passports. That time he decided to nationalize the Uganda British American Tobacco (BAT) Company's processing plants and went on to assert that he bought the BAT Company because the owners, along with the Asian community, were sabotaging the economy. He had given a 90-day bombastic notice for Asians to leave Uganda after accusing them of sabotaging the economy of Uganda and declaring that he wanted the economy of Uganda to be in the hands of Ugandan citizens, especially Black Ugandans. This very first "very public" "bad behavior" had happened barely two years into Dad's rule in Uganda and a little over a year to the month in July 1971 when he received a very warm welcome from Britain during his first official foreign trip as President of Uganda.

It was as if Dad wanted to spite British Newspapers that had sung his praises and "screamed" "insults" at his predecessor Apollo Milton Obote immediately following the Military Coup that catapulted him to the position of President of Uganda. It was also as if Dad wanted to take it upon himself to mete out punishment to the British for the "sins" of the colonialism the Organization of African Unity he addressed in May 1973 aimed to redress.

As outlined in a previous section, following the Coup against Apollo Milton Obote on January 25, 1971, in London, England, The Daily Telegraph editorial had this headline:

"Good Riddance to Obote", while The Times had observed that the reign of Obote "was no longer worth protecting." It had added that Obote's government had been " — hostile to British interests [sales of arms to South Africa], contemptuous of Europeans... ethnically divisive and potentially so unpopular that no British Government would be able to shore it up, let alone wish to be associated with it."

In February 1971, Dad's stand against communism had been hailed in The Daily Telegraph. A caption had read, "from Africa, one commonsense voice has come through loud and clear, and it is that of General (now President) Amin, who assured that Uganda would certainly not leave the Commonwealth."

CHAPTER SIX

On February 2, 1971, the British Government of Edward Heath had formally recognized Dad's government.

After his ascent to the "highest position in the land" of Uganda and a "honeymoon" period with Britain, instead of conforming to "expectations" intimated in the British Newspapers and continuing to bask in their "praises", Dad seemed to want to do the total opposite! He seemed to have had a total change of heart towards Britain. He declared war on "Imperialism" instead and Uganda's Asian community became a pawn and the first to be unwittingly caught in the crossfire!

Dad started advocating for and implementing the very same policies and plans that had "alienated" his predecessor Apollo Milton Obote from Britain and led to the British Newspapers "insulting" him, following the Coup against him in the first place. It started to become clear that Dad was not going to live up to what Britain and others who allegedly "hand-picked" him to replace Apollo Milton Obote "expected".

By May 1973 when Dad attended and addressed the OAU Summit in Addis Ababa, Ethiopia, he had made a 180-degree turn against Britain. After the "thunderous" cheers he received from inside and outside the Africa Hall during the OAU Summit in Addis Ababa, Ethiopia, Dad seemed very eager to use his position as President of an "Independent" African country, to champion and take the cause of the OAU to a new level!

Like a "bad marriage" waiting to end in a divorce, Dad seemed to want Uganda to be completely independent from Britain while "needing" Britain's "approval" at the same time. He never stopped reminiscing about his Kings African Rifles days and "bragging" about being part of the Guard Patrol when news came through in Kenya of the death of Queen Elizabeth II's father King George VI and her ascension to the British Throne in 1952. He never stopped talking about his close friendships with British Superiors in the Kings African Rifles and the mutual respect and admiration they had for each other.

However, many times, Dad would fondly refer to the British as loyal friends of Uganda while also "berating" them for colonizing Uganda, parts of Africa and many countries of the African Diaspora. It was always confusing to listen to him praising the British while also "taunting" them every time an opportunity presented itself - like the time Britain experienced "economic challenges" in 1973.

The 1974 French Film Documentary on Dad

In 1974, the French Documentary made about Dad titled, "General Idi Amin Dada: A Self Portrait" was shown extensively around the world. During the making of the film, Dad made statements that were taken out of context. Several of his statements were labeled as nonsensical. However, they came to pass.

In the Documentary, Dad made a lot of "audacious" statements such as:

"The Black people of America must be the President of the United States of America". "They must be the Secretary of State."

This is because he wanted all people of African Descent to feel confident and proud of their heritage and he succeeded in doing so for Ugandans.

Dad's predictions and so-called "nonsensical ramblings" regarding an African American President and Secretary of State came to pass!

He always mouthed that "Black people are more brilliant than any other race". He did this to the horror of people who worried that such statements would lead to additional backlash against him and other Ugandans but he didn't care about making such "audacious" statements "on camera".

Many of Dad's statements have been labeled nonsensical because he conveyed them in English - a language he didn't care for but was "forced" to communicate in because of colonialism. Dad was very eloquent, very articulate and very fluent in a number of African languages and if he was afforded the opportunity to convey his statements in one of these languages, his statements would have had the clarity he intended.

The 1974 French Documentary and other films about Dad will be great additions to the background information for the section of the series titled "Other People Speak", along with other material relating to the debate about whether Dad was a hero or villain to the core. A discussion is encouraged as the series, Idi Amin: Hero or Villain? His Son Jaffar Amin and Other People Speak unfolds!

CHAPTER SEVEN

Events in neighbouring countries and a coup

As Dad continued to hang onto power amidst the sabotage and propaganda intended to bring him down, he continued to follow events in neighbouring countries.

Earlier in 1974, there had been a visit to Juba, Southern Sudan by the Emperor Haile Selassie of Ethiopia, to celebrate the Anniversary of the signing of the Addis Ababa Accord and continuing peace in the Sudan, which Dad was instrumental in bringing about.

Emperor Haile Selassie of Ethiopia had arrived in Juba the Capital of Southern Sudan to celebrate the Anniversary of the signing of the Addis Ababa Accord, which he had witnessed in March 1972. The colourful event was attended by hordes of crowds that were hopeful about the continuing peace in the Sudan.

Meanwhile, a rift had developed between Dad and Senior Christian Army Officers from Dad's Kakwa tribe, which had led to a coup against Dad in January 1974. According to Dad, two issues created the rift, with the first being Dad's broken relationship with Israel after being a loyal friend, strong supporter and ally for years and fathering twins with an Israeli Secret Service

(Mossad) Agent. The second issue was the integration and appointment of Sudanese Anyanya in top positions following the signing of the Addis Ababa Accord in 1972.

Dad claimed that deep down the Christian Kakwas felt he made a wrong choice where the Israelis were concerned. He claimed that they felt that he should have kept what to them was a watertight engagement with the battle hardened Israelis to the very end - much in the mould of the Warrior Kakwas of old.

According to Dad, this factor came to a head in January 1974, when three Battle Hardened Kakwa Christian Army Officers along with a Justice plotted a mutiny against him. They were Charles Arube from the Kakwa clan of Kaliwara in Ko'buko (Ko'boko), Elly Aseni from the Kakwa clan of Godiya in Ko'buko (Ko'boko), Isaac Lumago from the Kakwa clan of Isoko in Ko'buko (Ko'boko) and Justice Opu from the Kakwa clan of Ludara in Ko'buko (Ko'boko). According to Dad, the four Kakwa Christian Army Officers probably acted under instructions from either the Soviets or even the Israeli Mossad, leading to the attempted coup in January 1974.

The rift that developed between Dad and the Senior Christian Army Officers from his Kakwa tribe over his decision to appoint Sudanese Anyanya in top positions following the signing of the Addis Ababa Accord would persist and contribute to his downfall in April 1979.

According to Dad, the issue mainly centered on the Sudanese Anyanya I contingent that he absorbed into the Uganda Army following the end of the First Sudanese War in 1972. Since the "warring factions" had just signed a Peace Agreement in Addis Ababa, the Indigenous soldiers felt affronted by the presence of Sudanese in top positions. Examples included Moses Ali, Lieutenant Colonel Malera, Gore, Taban Lupayi and others. The fact that most of them were top Flight Officers who got their training in Great Britain and Israel was secondary to their concerns.

Dad said the involvement of Justice Opu in the coup attempt pointed to Constitutional concerns about the prevalence of Kenyans, Tanzanians, Rwandese Tutsi, Sudanese and Congolese in the Security Services. The likes of Isaac Maliyamungu were most likely to bring in contingents of Congolese Kakwa from Jaki County in the Congo. Taban Lupayi would bring in Pojulu from the Sudan. Moses Ali brought in Bari from the Sudan.

Dad and his associates used to joke that the Rwandese Tutsis emptied out of the Refugee Camps and into the officers' homes as wives and their brothers ended up being recruited into the security services as far back as 1968. "This was by design!" they intimated.

Following is a sketchy outline of the attempted coup against Dad by Charles Arube, Elly Aseni, and Isaac Lumago, the three Battle Hardened Kakwa Christian Army Officers from Dad's Kakwa tribe as recounted by Dad:

Exactly three years to the time of the coup that catapulted Dad to power on January 25, 1971, there was a rumoured attempted coup by Charles Arube the Army Chief of Staff, that occurred between January 23 and 24, 1974. Arube was allegedly angry that in his absence in Moscow, a Muslim was put in his place. He was referring to the appointment of Lieutenant Colonel Malera who is an Animist and not a Muslim. Colonel Malera was one of the Sudanese soldiers absorbed into the Uganda Army following the end of the First Sudanese War.

I once asked Dad what could have turned Arube a close family member against him and Dad's answer was painful to hear. He re-enacted his phone call to Arube during which he asked Arube why Arube felt the need to take power from him.

According to Dad, Arube answered him that it was better for an educated Christian Kakwa to rule Uganda. According to Dad, he then proceeded to remind Arube of how close Arube's family was to ours and how he looked out for Arube and our uncle Luka and treated them like his own blood brothers. Dad reminded Arube that he promoted Arube to the position of Chief of Staff, in memory and recognition of his family relation with us.

"After all this, how can you turn against me surely?" Dad had concluded the phone conversation.

With tears in his eyes, Dad claimed that he then called our uncle Luka who had just returned from Libya to set up the Uganda Marines Corps at Bugolobi Barracks.

In July 1971, Dad had daringly left his 6-month regime in the capable but young hands of Sandhurst trained Brigadier General Charles Arube when some insurgents tried to storm the King George IV Garrison in Jinja. So he was disappointed that Charles Arube broke their trust and tried to take over the Uganda government from him through a Military Coup.

According to Dad, it was after a training course in the USSR that Charles Arube attempted to take over leadership from him through the Military Coup in January 1974 in connivance with Dad's uncle Elly Aseni, Justice Opu and Isaac Lumago. This would be a Christian Kakwa inspired coup attempt that was precipitated by dissatisfaction with the way Dad severed relationships with Israel and how Lieutenant Colonel Malera one of the Sudanese brought into Dad's army was handling the command of the Military Police.

Dad told us that during the mutiny instigated against him by the Senior Christian Army Officers from his Kakwa tribe, our uncle Luka kept insisting on knowing his location and where he was. However, Dad insisted that Luka take his Crack Marine Troopers and secure the key locations which had been taken over by troops loyal to Charles Arube, Elly Aseni and Isaac Lumago, again, all Christian Kakwas.

It was only after uncle Luka came back to Dad with affirmative confirmation of having retaken the capital that Dad was able to inform him that he was at the Makindye Lodge overlooking the city. Dad claimed that he could see Armoured Personnel Carriers roaming the streets of Kampala at the height of the attempted Coup D'etat.

This was an incident that raised concern among Temezi (Elders) from the Kakwa tribe because for generations, Blood Ties have taken precedence over Religious Ties in the Kakwa tribe. Dad just felt that Charles Arube had been influenced from "outside" by the British, Russians and the Israeli Mossad. He was convinced that Charles Arube, Elly Aseni, Isaac Lumago and Justice Opu would never have wanted him dead if they had not been influenced by "outsiders."

The Foreign Press reported that up to 30 Kakwa soldiers were killed at Makindye including Brigadier General Charles Arube, soon after returning from a Training Mission in Moscow with Isaac Lumago. However, there are also unconfirmed but undisputed accounts relating to suspicions that Charles Arube committed suicide by self-inflicting a gunshot wound after realizing the consequences of the mutiny and coup he and the other Senior Christian Army Officers from Dad's Kakwa tribe had instigated. An Independent Truth and Reconciliation Commission is also the place to arrive at the actual truth about events surrounding Charles Arube's sad and untimely death.

According to Dad, even if Arube urgently wanted him killed, he had underestimated both the powers that he had over the soldiers and his personal courage. Indeed, Dad, dressed in his pajamas, immediately came out and spoke to the soldiers, ordering them to unload their weapons and return to the barracks. He then put on his uniform, got into his own vehicle and drove to all the trouble spots where peace was quickly restored. It was a typical display of his innate leadership and fearlessness in the face of adversity.

According to reliable sources, Elly Aseni was spared the wrath of the irate soldiers because he came from Dad's Paternal Uncles the Godiya Kakwa clan. Following the coup attempt, he was magnanimously given the Ambassadorship of the USSR by Dad while Isaac Lumago was eventually given the Ambassadorship of Lesotho. Rumours abound about Isaac Lumago's father approaching my Grandpa Amin Dada Nyabira and the two of them together talking to Dad about sparing Lumago's life.

According to Dad, he sent the people from his own Kakwa tribe for Specialist Training abroad but they would come back from Russia or the United States of America thinking they were better educated than him and start getting ideas that they wanted to rule. Dad said that the superpowers started creating tensions between him and his trusted Lieutenants to get at him.

During Dad's rule in Uganda, there were constant threats of coups. However, he said that he stamped down on these coups because he had a very good intelligence service that had been set up by the United States of America and the USSR and before that by the Israelis and the British.

In 1974, Lieutenant Colonel Hussein Malera, Commanding Officer of the Military Police in Makindye was ordered out of Uganda to the Sudan his birthplace by Dad. Originally from the Baka tribe in the Yei River District, Lieutenant Colonel Malera left Uganda for the Sudan in a massive convoy of cars and trucks. The trek was a spectacle to behold and Dad's associates regularly recounted circumstances surrounding the "deportation" ordered by Dad.

CHAPTER SEVEN

The sentence to death of Denis Hills

Events that unfolded in May and June 1975 in relation to the arrest and trial of Denis Hills, a British Sociology Lecturer at Makerere University, Uganda would go down in history as some of the most memorable events that occurred during Dad's rule in Uganda. The situation was made worse by the fact that Dad's relationship with Britain had become "strained" after a series of "bad behaviours" by Dad towards Britain and its citizens and a "disappointing" turn of events where Britain's "expectations" of Dad were concerned. Dad seemed to be giving Britain and the other parties who allegedly "hand picked" him to replace Apollo Milton Obote a run for their money with his "unexpected" "waywardness"! Nevertheless, Britain continued maintaining Diplomatic Relations with Uganda, its former colony.

Opinions abound as to why Britain continued a "strained" relationship with an "ungovernable" Dad and these opinions are recommended readings for the section of the series titled "Other People Speak", along with other background information. However, despite the "bad behaviours" Dad exhibited after the "honeymoon" period with Britain, many British citizens continued to reside and offer their services in Uganda including Denis Hills, the British Sociology Lecturer at Makerere University.

According to various reports, Denis Hills was arrested, tried by a Military Tribunal and found guilty of treason for his book "The White Pumpkin", which is critical of Dad and his regime and the initial Book Manuscript described Dad as a "pagan tyrant". To many British citizens Dad was no longer the 'Gentle Giant' "they" "praised", immediately following the Military Coup against his predecessor Apollo Milton Obote in January 1971. Like Denis Hills, they exercised their right to free speech and didn't shy away from voicing their negative opinions about Dad. However, for Denis Hills, his right to free speech and voicing opinions about Dad would become a nightmare that would haunt him for a very long time.

According to reports, Dad's intelligence got word of the contents of Denis Hills' initial Book Manuscript and arrested him. It is reported that Denis Hills was first acquitted of all charges by a Ugandan Magistrate but later tried by a Military Tribunal that found him guilty of treason and sentenced him to death by firing squad on June 21, 1975. The reference to Dad by Denis Hills as a "pagan tyrant" was what precipitated the charge of treason against him.

The British Government panicked and sent Lieutenant General Sir Chandos Blair and Dad's former Commanding Officer Iain Grahame to plead for clemency. According to reports, Queen Elizabeth II sent Dad a personal appeal to spare

Denis Hills' life. Dad seized this as another "perfect" opportunity to "taunt" Britain and its citizens "for the sins of colonialism."

Upon arriving in Uganda, the two envoys Lieutenant General Sir Chandos Blair and Dad's former Commanding Officer Iain Grahame proceeded to Arua to meet Dad. They were accompanied by Colonel Sabuni, one of Dad's officers. Dad was very open to the meeting with the two British envoys but he had "something up his sleeve!"

Iain Grahame described what happened next:

"Bucking low to avoid the thatch (Amin's hut), we entered as instructed kneeling before the President. Inside, a quite remarkable sight greeted our eyes. Close to the opening was a two-man television crew one of whom was holding a battery operated light that was directed towards the far end of the hut. There sitting on an enormous curved wooden throne was his Excellency the President of Uganda. He was wearing the largest Mexican sombrero that I have ever seen, blue pinstripe bush jacket and trousers, a Christian Dior scarf and the inevitable size fourteen of brown shoes."

In Kakwa culture and other cultures of Uganda and Africa, kneeling before anyone is considered the utmost sign of reverence. It also occurs when someone is begging for mercy. Dad obviously set the scene described by Iain Grahame so that the two British citizens could "kneel before him".

I can only imagine how hard Dad must have laughed in private at the fact that he had successfully "duped" and "orchestrated" two Wazungu (White men) to "kneel before him". It would have been the very same tearful earthquake laugh he was engaged in when he played the "African Chili Prank" on my siblings and I the day he offered us chili laden roast chicken after noticing our keen interest in the chicken. It had been the very first time several of my siblings and I got to know Dad and began living in his official residences as the President's Children. That time, we didn't find Dad's "African Chili Prank" as funny as he thought it was and the two British envoys may not have found the deliberate "set up" by Dad for them to "kneel before him" funny either.

During the meeting between Dad and the two British envoys Lieutenant General Sir Chandos Blair and Dad's former Commanding Officer Iain Grahame, he presented Lieutenant General Blair with assorted bows and arrows and Iain Grahame with the musical instrument, Nanga. He also gave Lieutenant General Blair the manuscript of Denis Hills' book. That day, Dad entertained Lieutenant General Blair and Iain Grahame to a typical Kakwa delicacy of bowels of goat meat, kon'ga (edible white ants) and "the skin of some

CHAPTER SEVEN 99

lungfish [popularly known in the West Nile by the name aboke] from the Nile."

Iain Grahame commented, "I made a bee-line for the ants, one of my favourite traditional African delicacies."

On June 10, 1975, Dad stipulated six conditions that had to be fulfilled before Denis Hills could be spared the firing squad:

"The British stop all malicious propaganda against me, the Government and the people of Uganda mounted in Britain and international news media. Expel all Uganda exiles presently in Britain who are spreading unfounded rumours against Uganda. The British media must stop their fruitless campaigns against Uganda by trying to persuade other friendly countries not to give any technical or other material assistance to Uganda and at the same time trying to persuade potential tourists not to come to Uganda. Stop and desist from making wild and useless reports that Uganda is in a state of chaos."

Dad's concerns were confirmed by the fact that while attending the Commonwealth Conference in Kingston, Jamaica, the British Prime Minister himself made some unfortunate reference that Uganda could not afford to host the forthcoming summit of the OAU (Organization of African Unity) Heads of State and Government.

"They must be prepared to sell to Uganda all the spare parts of military equipment which

Uganda bought from Britain, such as Saladin armoured cars and Ferret scout cars, and any other spare parts for British military hardware bought by Uganda. The British Prime Minister or the Queen, who is the Head of the Commonwealth, must give me a written confirmation of the conditions enumerated above and the Defence Council has directed that this confirmation must reach Kampala ten days from tomorrow".

The spectacle deliberately set up by Dad that involved Lieutenant General Sir Chandos Blair and Iain Grahame "kneeling before him" as they bucked low to avoid Dad's thatch became a standing joke among Ugandans as they laughed about Dad's "audacity" to continue "taunting" their former colonial masters. Some Ugandans laughed even harder as they regularly recalled Dad pulling off yet another "stunt" by "setting up" fourteen Ex-Services British men who joined the Uganda Army to "kneel before him" as they "pledged" to take up arms for Uganda. Many Ugandans thought the spectacles were funny but others found them in terrible taste!

The spectacles involving Lieutenant General Sir Chandos Blair and Iain Grahame "kneeling before Dad" and the very public "reverence" and "declaration of loyalty" by fourteen Ex-Services British men who joined the Uganda Army in a so-called "pledge" were jokes Dad mocked in private as he laughed hard!

No one needed to kneel to "pledge" to take up arms for Uganda. Dad just wanted to "reverse" the Master-Servant "roles" that existed between the British and Ugandans because of colonialism. As I stated before, in Kakwa culture and other cultures of Uganda and Africa, kneeling before anyone is considered the utmost sign of reverence.

"Idi Amin wanted to humiliate a couple of White British citizens as 'punishment' for the 'sins' of colonialism and the African Slave Trade, which Britain participated in before 'championing' its end," many people have intimated.

It would be interesting to hear what others have to say about the spectacles and the reasons why fourteen Ex-Services British men joined the Uganda Army in the first place and endured the "humiliation" Dad subjected them to. There will be opportunities for related discussions as the series Idi Amin: Hero or Villain? His Son Jaffar Amin and Other People Speak unfolds.

According to accounts, in July 1975, General Mobutu of Zaire (Congo) and others urged Dad to hand over Denis Hills into the hands of the British Foreign Secretary James Callaghan in Kampala. Present at this historic moment and hand over was Jim Hennessy, the British Ambassador in Uganda at the time. Before the formal hand over to James Callaghan, Denis Hills had to apologize fully to the President of Uganda - Dad.

At the Command Post, one of Dad's residences and in front of Representatives of the British Press, Lieutenant General Sir Chandos Blair and Iain Grahame drank large quantities of Uganda's favourite alcoholic drink, Uganda Waragi. Their actions later gave rise to a jest throughout Uganda's bars, schools and other places of social gathering.

Instead of asking for a Waragi, Ugandans would simply ask for a "Double Blair" or "Neat Blair". The local press also reported that after gulping down so much Waragi, Lieutenant General Blair was too drunk to walk, so he had to be supported.

CHAPTER EIGHT

Dad as Chairman of the OAU

Between July 28, 1975 and August 1, 1975, the Organization of African Unity (OAU) Summit took place in Kampala and Dad was Chairman. He organized and made the Summit into such a colourful event that many of his associates and other Ugandans "bragged" about it for a very long time.

Prior to the Summit, there were construction projects all over the place as Dad wanted to make a lasting impression on delegates. Some of the resulting projects include the present day Conference Centre and the Serena Hotel (Formerly Nile Mansions Hotel). During the OAU Summit, delegates laughed as Dad repeatedly said, "I was born on this very spot". Many thought that Dad was at his usual pranks and jests but he was dead serious this time because he was indeed born at the very location of the Conference Centre and the Serena Hotel (Formerly the Nile Mansions Hotel) in Kampala in 1928.

Despite Dad's sincere attempt to tell delegates to the Organization of African Unity Summit, "I was born on this very spot", a lot of the media and even Ugandans dismissed this fact as another "wayward" attempt by Dad to be funny.

Dad liked to jest but he was very serious in asserting that he was born at the location of the International Conference Centre in Kampala and Nile Mansions Hotel.

To this day, many people cannot imagine the Kampala of the 1920s, let alone the fact that Dad's parents lived there that time and he was born at the very location of the International Conference Centre and the Nile Mansions Hotel in Kampala.

In the same year 1975, Dad married Sarah Kyolaba a so-called go-go dancer from the Suicide Mechanized Unit Jazz Band in Masaka. The marriage was a lavish affair televised over Uganda Television and it coincided with the OAU Summit in Uganda that was chaired by Dad. The Reception was held at the same location and hall where the OAU Summit was held. Many associates of Dad's and Ugandans remembered the lavish reception for a long time. The Palestine Liberation Organization's (PLO's) Yasser Arafat was the Best Man at Dad and Sarah Kyolaba's wedding. There are claims that Dad married Sarah the Islamic way then he was forced to repeat the Wedding during the OAU Summit.

I have recollections of many dignitaries hosted by Dad and will always remember the time The Nation of Islam dignitaries came to Uganda on Dad's invitation during the OAU Summit in 1975.

Mobutu, with all his Afro-Jazz Bands and the likes of Mpongo Love, Orchestra Veve and Orchestra Lipua Lipua, Pure Raz Mataz impressed me a great deal! This is because like most Ugandans, I loved Congolese Music as a child. I still do and believe that it is one of the best demonstrations of African talent. Dad couldn't get enough of it!

"Black Empowerment" and Arab Groups

The state visits by "Black Empowerment Groups", including The Nation of Islam under Louis Farrakhan (based in the USA), The Black Panthers (based in the USA), the PLO and other Arab Nationalist Groups during the 1975 OAU were among the most memorable occasions that occurred in 1975.

Dad's invitation to "Black Empowerment Groups", originating from the United States of America was for purposes of his agenda to call on the Black Peoples in the American Diaspora to unite. He emphasized unity for Black people way back, just as he was uniting the Frontline States against Apartheid and their perceived notion that Israel was an Apartheid state too, which won him the landslide UN Resolution 3379 between 1975-1992 that I write about in a section below.

That year 1975, the Leader of The Nation of Islam, Elijah Muhammad died and one Abdul

Haleem Farrakhan was the one who led the delegation to Uganda for the OAU Summit in Kampala in place of Wallace. Many people couldn't get over how The Nation of Islam dignitaries came to Uganda on Dad's invitation during the OAU Summit when something like that had never been done before. However, Dad had an agenda to unite Black people in the United States of America and the OAU afforded an opportunity for him to implement that agenda.

Dad was obsessed with liberating African people everywhere from oppression. He never stopped asserting that African people everywhere needed to be liberated. For example, he continued to constantly rave about how "the Black people of America must be the President of the United States of America" and how they "must be the Secretary of State." It is a statement he repeated "on camera" in the 1974 French Documentary titled "General Idi Amin Dada: A Self Portrait."

Fond memories of the bald Black American

I still remember and have fond memories of the bald cameraman with the beautiful bride-to-be. They were part of Louis Farrakhan's entourage to the OAU Summit in Uganda in 1975.

That time, Dad lined us his children at Nile Mansions Hotel (Serena Hotel) and went through a formal introduction of all of us. The beautiful lady who had on the original Whoopi Goldberg beads 1970s style - way before Whoopi showed up on the radar screen in 1975, repeatedly asked with marked wonder:

"All your children?"

"Yes" responded Dad.

I was at the very end of the row and I could see the bald-headed husband-to-be grinning from ear to ear, right next to her. It is funny that I ended up with the very same Isaac Hayes close shave.

In 1989, while living in exile in Saudi Arabia, I asked Louis Farrakhan's Chief of Staff about this golden couple after running into Louis Farrakhan and his entourage in Saudi Arabia. Even Dad was surprised at how I could remember the event with The Nation of Islam dignitaries.

I told Dad that it was because of the groom's bald head - a style I wear today. They actually got married either in Uganda or Morocco. The two lovebirds actually traversed the country filming. I pray I can get footages of their travels, for they kept taking photos of the whole "brood" - priceless Colour Photos in 1975.

We got used to Technicolour way back, as per the coloured pictures Dad was fond of taking with his favourite Maroon Leather Embossed Aluminum Polaroid Camera.

By the time the satellite was up and running at Mpoma, Kololo, Soroti and Ombaci Relay Stations, Dad had brought in the earliest versions of Toshiba Colour Televisions. He had also brought in Sony Video Decks and the works, from Dubai.

Actually my paternal uncle Ramadhan Amin and his Pakistani associate Abdul Sattar were the pioneers of the Dubai route for Dad's Uganda Airlines plied the route. It still had the concession under the Monika QU (Uganda Airlines) with direct flights to Jeddah, Riyadh, Dubai, Abu Dhabi, Kuwait City, Karachi and other places and for the record Dad actually acquired the pioneer versions of Cellular Telephones, which prompted his number to be changed from 2241 to 20241.

Dad traversed the country with the colloquially called Simu Ya Upepu (air phone or what is termed wireless). He was fond of gadgets.

A spear throwing jest with American friends

The scene of the bald cameraman with the beautiful bride-to-be who was part of Louis Farrakhan's entourage asking Dad if we were all his kids was also the same scene where Dad playfully hurtled towards the cameraman with a spear and launched it at his feet in jest. I remember the day very well because the cameraman actually brought down his camera to nervously look at where the spear had landed.

That time, the whole 30 yard line up of children laughed with glee, knowing Dad was up to no good as usual but also show-bouting to his Black American friends and the OAU dignitaries. I was present that day and witnessed Dad's mischief as he show-bouted to his Black American friends and the OAU dignitaries and regularly reflected on what was going on in their minds as they interacted with Dad. That time, Dad also wanted to demonstrate Acholi dances, which he loved.

Dad's "spear throwing" jest and other interactions with dignitaries to the OAU Summit in Kampala that year were shown on colour televisions across the world. He realized that it was his chance to show-bout progress. This was the very time he got the Pioneer Cellular Telephone that was relayed to the earth station in Mpoma, Kololo and Ombaci and across the world, while the Nakasero and Soroti Relay Radio Stations relayed radio across the world. The Green Channel was the very first FM Radio Station.

Dad was great as a father. He was proud of us his children and he loved to show us off to dignitaries. He accepted, gathered and took care of all of us, including ones born out of wedlock like me.

I share details about Dad as a father in another project titled "My Father Idi Amin Was Daddy To Us: Jaffar Amin Speaks In Memoirs,

Reflections And Spoken Words", along with the dynamics of growing up in a household with more than one mother.

An inversion of roles

Ugandans who were at hand at the time will never forget the day in 1975 during the Organization of African Unity (OAU) Summit when Dad orchestrated an "inversion of roles". That day, Bob Astles, Dad's friend and ex-Royal Engineer on which the fictional character Nicholas Garrigan in the hit movie "The Last King of Scotland" is loosely based and a couple of European businessmen living in Uganda at the time carried Dad to a Reception on a litter. One of the businessmen was a British named Robert Scanlon.

In this exercise, a Swede walked behind with a parasol, a long stick that he held over Dad's head, while Bob Astles walked alongside the group. What a spectacle it was! Caucasian men, carrying a Black African! A hilariously true inversion of roles!

The Caucasians in this jestful event were also laughing because they were not forced to carry Dad. They did it willingly.

Relishing the opportunity to showcase Uganda

During the 1975 Organization of African Unity Summit in Kampala, Dad relished the opportunity to showcase Uganda as a very beautiful country. He gave dignitaries to the Summit a tour of Ugandan landmarks and interesting features, including a statue erected in his honour.

The statue was placed on the grounds of the Cape Town Villas Hotel. Like Saddam Hussein's statue during the Iraqi War, it was smashed to the ground after Dad's government was overthrown in 1979.

While the festivities of the Organization of African Unity (OAU) Summit were taking place in Kampala, Uganda, Yakubu Gowon, Head of State of Nigeria at the time got a call that Murtala Mohammed had taken over power in a Military Coup in Nigeria. Like Apollo Milton Obote before Dad, he too would be forced to live in exile.

Other dignitaries who attended the OAU Summit in Kampala that year included President Bokassa of the Central African Republic.

Dad's obsession with piling on the medals came after the visit by President Bokassa during the OAU Summit in 1975. That is when those funny round and flowerish medals from the Arab Islamic countries started appearing just below the neat row of British Accolades. He used to just have the Israeli Paratrooper Wings and a multi colour cloth parchment accolade. The "Arab Medals" first started "popping up" post the 1973 Arab - Israeli war.

The Arabs had seen Dad's commitment during the 1973 war between Israel and the Arab Islamic World. It was the very first time the Arabs united since the days of Salahudeen (Saladin).

Because of his unwavering support for the Arab people, the "Petrol Dollars" supported Dad's regime until his fall in 1979.

The participation of Uganda in the 1973 war against Israel when they suffered their only defeat against the combined Arab Islamic Nations brought Dad a lot of prestige and Honours from Arab countries.

The Medals started to pile up and the incessant Tours of the OIC (Organisation of Islamic Conference) countries rolled. Every reception was concluded with the award of the highest accolades, which Dad insisted on sticking onto his No.1 Military Dressage Coat.

The Nubi (Nubians) gave Dad the Pet name (Abu Jarara) meaning Father of Buttons in Kinubi, the language of the Nubi (Nubians).

The Western Media laughed at the spectacle but like the typical WWII "Red Poppy" day in England where Veterans proudly wear the "Red Poppy", Dad continued to wear his buttons given by Arab countries and he didn't care about being ridiculed. For he had an Islamic constituency he was well aware of and he cultivated the Network.

Today we Muslims stand at 1.5 Billion and we are expected to reach 2 Billion by 2020.

Dad was playing to a gallery and both sides knew the count, the casualties and the honors won or lost.

Dad's clarity at the 1975 OAU Summit

As Dad did in previous Organization of African Unity (OAU) Summits, he was very clear in articulating his messages relating to Africa and the Diasporas - True Independence for all "Peoples of Africa", self sufficiency, the need to come together and etc, etc. As the Chair that year, Dad was as bombastic as ever during the 1975 OAU Summit in Kampala and he "walked the talk!" It is worth mentioning that a number of significant events occurred in 1975 during his tenure as Chairman of the OAU, namely the successful Emancipation of five African countries.

During the year 1975, the African countries of Angola, Cape Verde, Comoros, Mozambique, Sao Tome and Principe gained "Independence" under Dad's Chairmanship, in fulfillment of his "Dream Speech" at the OAU Summit in May 1973 in Addis Ababa, Ethiopia. Seychelles, Djibouti and Zimbabwe followed suit in 1976, 1977 and 1980 respectively. Interestingly Namibia and South

Africa were the only outstanding "Liberation Objectives" he did not achieve as he set out to do when he articulated a "Liberation Plan" during the articulate speech he gave at the OAU Summit held in Addis Ababa, Ethiopia in May 1973. However, I venture to say that his efforts contributed to Namibia gaining "Independence" in 1990 and Indigenous South Africans being freed from the shackles of Legalized Racism in 1994 at last!

Addressing the UN and Resolution 3379

In November 1975 Dad travelled to New York to address the United Nations as Chairman of the OAU (Organization of African Unity) that year.

In a "flamboyant defiance and audacity" at the Airport in New York, Dad's favourite Dance Troupe "The Heart Beat of Afrika" danced for him! He had sent the Dance Troupe ahead of him so that they could dance for him, entertain and welcome him on American soil at the Airport, while "flaunting" the beauty and talent of Africa. This "flamboyant defiance and audacity" by Dad on American soil caused a lot of laughter, even though some people were annoyed by it.

Dad said it was his way of poking fun at the United States of America for the evils and "sins" of the African Slave Trade. He said he wanted to remind Americans that "Africans" are the brightest and most talented human beings on earth and they made and built the United States of America. So Americans better treat Black Americans better than they have been doing for centuries.

By the time Dad travelled to New York to address the United Nations in 1975, the once strong relationship he had with Israel had become irreparable. It had disintegrated beyond recognition.

As Chairman of the OAU (Organization of African Unity) in 1975, Dad addressed the United Nations in Luganda, one of many Ugandan languages he was very articulate and very eloquent in. On that occasion, he chose to defy United Nations rules respecting languages accepted as Official Languages at the United Nations and spoke in Luganda.

During Dad's speech at the United Nations in New York, he was very instrumental in passing UN Resolution 3379, equating Zionism with Racism and Apartheid.

The arising Resolution stood the Test of Time from 1975 to 1991 when George Bush Senior sought an Alliance to fight against Saddam Hussein. At the time of the passing of UN Resolution 3379, Africans came together as one to protect their "wayward" Chairman Dad.

Dad caused a murmur at the United Nations when he spoke in Luganda, a language he mastered while growing up among the Baganda people of Uganda. When he defiantly forced the Luganda language on the United Nations in New York in 1975 and gave an address in Luganda, he was very clear in articulating his points.

As Chairman of the Organization of African Unity that year, Dad felt it was necessary to clearly articulate his position at the United Nations in relation to UN Resolution 3379, without the constraints of language. He was always aware of his constituency.

He had already set up the International External Service of the Uganda Broadcasting Corporation and knew that the people that mattered were listening. Dad was speaking directly to his constituency and Luganda was actually the one language he spoke fluently. Even the Baganda were stupefied and elated to hear him speak their language on the world stage, for Swahili was the preeminent language - actually the only language with a translatable service at the United Nations.

Dad could also speak Swahili fluently but he chose to speak in Luganda. Many Baganda and other Ugandans cheered and laughed about Dad's "audacity" to force Luganda on the United Nations while other people were very annoyed by this form of "waywardness".

Younis Kinene, Uganda's Ambassador to the United Nations at the time had to be the "Impromptu Translator" for Luganda back to

English. I can only imagine what must have gone through Younis Kinene's head as his "wayward" Head of State put him in the awkward position of "Impromptu Translator", with no warning whatsoever.

Dad was making a statement. He understood the significance of the occasion and he did not wish to be compromised. He understood that he represented Africa at that moment as the Chairman of the OAU and he was aware of the significance of the occasion and necessity for eloquent articulation.

Dad's humble upbringing and crowd pleasing style resonated with the teeming masses. This style stemmed from his gift of speech. He had the astonishing ability to lead a Nation due to his extraordinary fluency in at least a dozen Indigenous African languages. His memory for words, for people and places never ceased to amaze his former Kings African Rifles Commanding Officer Major Iain Grahame. He spoke directly to the people in a language they understood. The essence of good communication in today's ICT generation is the ability to get your message across. This factor is quite often ignored by his detractors, but it is the most indelible testament as to why he continues to resonate with the majority of the now revived underclass ("Common Man") under this structurally adjusted society in the 21st century.

I would venture to say that Dad did very well in attempting to communicate in English. I doubt that many people would perform so well if they were "dumped" in a hostile environment and expected to pick up and communicate in a language they had no interest in learning or mastering. I know they would sound just as "nonsensical" to Native Speakers. However, the irony of Dad's so-called "nonsensical" statements is that they came to pass with the appointments of Colin Powell and Condoleezza Rice as United States Secretaries of State and the election of Barack Obama as President of the United States of America.

I am particularly referring to "audacious" statements Dad made during the making of the 1974 French Documentary titled "General Idi Amin Dada: A Self Portrait." He had boldly stated:

"The Black people of America must be the President of the United States of America".

"They must be the Secretary of State."

CHAPTER NINE

A tussle between bodyguards and an Assassin

At the United Nations in 1975, Dad articulated that Zionism was equal to Racism, in a 10-minute speech following a 90-minute speech by Younis Kinene, Uganda's Ambassador to the United Nations at the time.

Zacharia Fataki from Gulumbi, a descendant of the notorious Chief of Gulumbi was Dad's Bodyguard in 1975. He regularly recounted the story of a tussle with an assassin, who was armed and in a "no arms area". It was suspected that the assassin was attempting to assassinate Dad while on the trip to New York.

Idi Osman of the Lurunu Kakwa clan who was Uganda's Ambassador to the United States of America at the time can also provide detailed accounts.

Younis Kinene can provide further key accounts about the whole event including Dad's visit to New York, his speech to the United Nations and how Africans came together as one to protect their "wayward" Chairman Dad.

It was a strange solidarity indeed in light of the strong protest from the American Ambassador who was determined to put Dad in his place so to speak and in a bad light. Dad believed that the US

Ambassador was very upset because Dad managed to convince all the African States, the Soviet Bloc and South American countries to vote for UN Resolution 3379.

Support and preparation for UN Resolution 3379

Preparation for UN Resolution 3379 began long before the Organization of African Unity (OAU) Summit in Uganda. There were a lot of determined stakeholders involved in its passing. Hence there was a lot of support for it.

By the time the OAU Summit in Uganda came around, Dad had been promoted to Field Marshall - one of the highest positions in the Military. In 1971, he had been denied the position of OAU Chairman because of the Military Coup against Apollo Milton Obote. However, by 1975, he had built enough clout to be recognized as a formidable force in the passing of UN Resolution 3379.

The Prime Minister of Great Britain at the time declared during a Commonwealth Conference in Kingston, Jamaica that Uganda could not hold the OAU Summit that year. However, what he did not realize was that the Arab Islamic Countries were determined to pass UN Resolution 3379 and it involved galvanizing the "Third World States" into a Bloc Vote and putting their money where their mouths were. This was the Era of the

Petrol Dollar and Dad had become the de facto spokesperson. The Arab countries ensured that he was successful in facilitating the passing of UN Resolution 3379 because they wanted it passed.

Dad evidently responded to being the de facto spokesperson and the African countries closed ranks to give him the votes he needed along with a standing ovation in the World Assembly when he successfully passed UN Resolution 3379, equating Zionism with Racism. However, little did Dad know that this resounding success would precipitate the Hostage Saga popularly known as the "Entebbe Raid" that would occur in Uganda, nine months after the passing of UN Resolution 3379.

The Africans came together as one to protect their "wayward" Chairman and to demonstrate their support for the Organization of African Unity (OAU). It was a strange solidarity indeed in light of the strong protest from the American Ambassador who was determined to put Dad in his place and in bad light so to speak.

Dad's medals, honours and opposition to Israel

Like Kings African Rifles (KAR) of old, which he truly was, a misplaced sense of grandeur somehow got the better of Dad. For when he invited Bokassa in 1975 to come and lay the foundation stone for the Old Kampala Mosque and the

University of Islam at Enjeva, he was still leaving the Number One dress bereft of the grandiose medals he piled up post 1975. He had also become an "outcast" amongst the "Western World" so his trips were limited to the OIC (Organisation of Islamic Conference) countries. At every stop, Dad was given medals and honors, which he piled onto his suit jacket. In fact he would affectionately ask Mrs. Emilio Mondo to do the needful and sew them on for him. She once told her beloved daughter Esther Mondo:

"You see all those medals? I painstakingly sewed them all - the lot of them".

Dad's opposition to the Jewish State of Israel that he was once very close to could not have been any clearer when he lobbied hard, for the passing of UN Resolution 3379. As I stated in a preceding section, he became the de facto spokesperson for the Palestinian People and he did manage to successfully facilitate the passing of UN Resolution 3379 equating Zionism with Racism. However, nothing prepared him for the Hostage Saga popularly known as the "Entebbe Raid" which would occur nine months after the successful passing of UN Resolution 3379 and forever seal his fate in the age-old tussle between Abraham's children Ishmael and Isaac.

As fate would have it, the Saga would play itself right in Uganda and cost the lives of innocent Ugandans unwittingly caught in the crossfire and "dragged" into the age-old war between two warring factions determined to fight to the death to claim supremacy, legitimacy and land! As I alluded to in a previous section, the lines had been drawn when Dad ended his relationship with Israel and took up with the Arabs and the Ummah (Community of Muslim Believers).

I often wonder how Grandma Aisha Chumaru Aate would have responded to Dad's "unexpected" 180-degree turn against Israel and direct opposition to the Jewish State if she had been alive. I also wonder if Dad remembered her words to him regarding the children of God as she referred to the people of Israel.

As outlined in previous sections, Grandma had warned, "Do not forsake the children of God my son, never forsake the children of God." As Dad went about arguing and lobbying hard for the passing of UN Resolution 3379 at the world's highest assembly, I wonder if Grandma's words had "flashed" through his mind, even for a split second.

Opening Uganda House in New York and a tip

While in New York, Dad opened and commissioned Uganda House, a monument attributed to him. He had financed and built the 13 storey building from scratch in the world's Number 1 Business District. He had also bought Prime

Property around the world for Uganda and not for himself, including Prime Property in the United Kingdom, France and right next to the Vatican in Rome.

Upon Dad's return home from New York, he once told the family that the CIA had even the cleaning ladies as spies. He said he got fond of one Black American cleaning lady and gave her a very large tip. He had said to the lady, "I know you are suffering under the white man, but you have this. It will help you", while relishing the look of shock on the woman's face when he handed her 10,000 US dollars in cash!

The incident tickled Dad so much that he would laugh hard as he retold the story numerous times – his teary earth-quaking and chesty laughs.

Dad never got tired of reminiscing about that Waldorf-Astoria Hotel incident. The next time I saw the very hotel located in Manhattan was in the movie Trading Places, starring Eddie Murphy.

What went through my mind when I watched Trading Places was the grandeur of the place! It was a "Rags to Riches Story" of a Black man who made good. The story was similar to Dad's story - a former Kasanvu (coerced labourer) rising to the position of President of Uganda. Dad loved watching Trading Places and "enjoyed" the reversal of fortunes in the movie.

"Economic War" and an unusual encounter

As Dad reminisced about his successful trip to New York, Uganda's economy continued to deteriorate for ordinary Ugandans. During Dad's rule in Uganda, the economy deteriorated as a result of boycotts and economic sabotage by subversives. Issues that came up because of the economic sabotage and how they impacted ordinary Ugandans will be explored in subsequent parts of the series, Idi Amin: Hero or Villain? His Son Jaffar Amin and Other People Speak, along with other people's standpoints. However, following is an account relating to Dad's encounter with a "struggling" Ugandan.

Dad was out and about in the beige VW Registration Number UUU 017 when a motherly lady hailed the buggy and he stopped. She got in and asked to be dropped off at Kawempe Kiyindi Zone. On their way, she started to bitterly lament the effects of the "Economic War" on the citizens and concluded that Idi Amin Dada was a bad man.

Unbeknownst to her, she was lamenting directly to the very man incognito!

"There is no sugar, no salt and the basic minimum since the Indians left", lamented the motherly lady.

When they got to her homestead, her husband was at hand to welcome them in shock, knowing the famous UUU 017 buggy. He was surprised to see his wife come out of the famous buggy.

She thanked the driver profusely and took her groceries out of the front boot of the buggy.

Just as the mystery man drove off, the husband asked his wife, "Do you know the man who just dropped you off?"

"No but he is a very good man".

"That was the President of the country Idi Amin Dada."

"Mama Nyaboo nfudde!" the woman slumped to the ground in shock, lamenting of her impending death, in the Ganda language. She explained to her husband how she had lamented the state of affairs in the country not knowing she was talking to the very person she harangued. As a family they decided to vacate their house that very night and headed to their home village in Mubende.

Just as Dad got home, he called up Permanent Secretary Balinda to find out how he could help the lady acquire a business. Then a search party was sent to convey the good news only to find that the whole family had disappeared.

Dad insisted they be found and when the good news was explained to the neighbours, Dad's search party was able to locate the family.

To this day, the lady lives an affluent lifestyle but cannot for her life stop explaining the fear that went through her when she realized she had been insulting a whole President to his face.

I have been asked why Dad didn't identify himself to the woman and why he wasn't upset. I have also been asked if the "subversive elements" in the State Research Bureau who Dad said were "colluding" with the Ugandan exiles would have killed this lady and her family if they had been privy to this incident, to continue to "smear" his reputation and make it look like he ordered the deaths as he said. Here is what I have to say:

We are discussing the Platinum lining of how Dad ruled. He had a private side, which a lot of people saw. This private side should not be mixed with the propaganda efforts that truly buried his reputation. I noted that in the CTV interview I gave after the release of the hit movie "The Last King of Scotland". He had a simple way of dealing with his subjects.

Every Muslim who has been to Madrasa studies which starts at the age of 4 onwards will tell you of Khalifa Al Rashid who used to go around his Empire incognito and hear the problems of the masses, then come back and institute changes during the Caliphate of Baghdad.

People claim we do not have an ideology but we do - not Nubian but Islamic. "Lowu kana murran isma kalam" ("However bitter the words, listen to my words"), is a common saying in Islam.

We are sincere and sincerity is a virtue. That is what kept Dad in power, for even his very tribes mates, the Kakwas were plotting his downfall, based on the factor Nubian Kakwas and Baris said "Uwo agara weni?" ("In which school did he study?").

Dad once lamented that with the Embargo, the "Economic War" was a harder war to win than say the success of the 1972 "Mutukula Invasion".

Today the famous Registration Number UUU 017 has turned up in the hands of the brightest prospects in the Ugandan Music Industry. Maurice Kiirya is the proud owner of the Registration Number UUU 017 and wherever he goes with the famous buggy the old folks ask him where he got the Field Marshall's car from. They all seem to know it from memory and in a sense it shows that they were aware of his movements but no one tried to harm him except the Ugandan exiles and the "subversive elements" they "planted" inside Uganda.

Dad used to consistently say, "I do not need security, the citizens will protect me". He repeated this statement several times between 1971 and 1979, especially after the "Nsambia Grenade Attack". He believed in Patriotism for what it was worth.

Dad was a Nationalist at heart. He loved our culture, our traditions and the way we dress. He knew that true Independence is the act of releasing the country from the harness and shackles of colonialism and slavery. He was fully aware that given a chance, the Indigenous people can take up responsibility and full ownership of our country.

Dad gave his famous telephone line 2241-20241 to everyone and actually, he had the Pioneer Cellular Telephone 20241 from Marubeni or some Japanese firm, which he drove around with in his Maserati. He was on tap to anyone who sought his help and was fond of turning up at village funeral vigils or parties, uninvited.

The man knew each and every nook and cranny of the country he ruled and traversed it without Escorts. He moved around in his Beetle VW car with Registration Number UUU 017. For long distance trips, he had the Bell Agusta Helicopter PAW 01 and 02 with which he moved around to distant places like Kigezi and Karamoja.

Dad would request all the doctors to assemble at a specific time, ask them to list their names at the door, find out their needs and respond immediately. Some doctors missed out on brand new cars because they thought the ubiquitous list was a "death list". Some still lament for they had written fictitious names and could not then come up and claim their prize.

The chickens associated with opposition to Israel

As if the evil and unconscionable "disappearance" of Kenyan Makerere University student Esther Chesire and murders of Ugandans Paul Sserwanga and Mrs. Theresa Nanziri Mukasa-Bukenya were not enough, barely one week following the brutal murder of Mrs. Bukenya and her unborn baby on June 23, 1976, something unexpected happened. The chickens associated with Dad's opposition to the Jewish State of Israel came home to roost!

As outlined in a previous section, Dad's opposition to the Jewish State of Israel that he was once very close to could not have been any clearer when he lobbied hard, for the passing of UN Resolution 3379 at the United Nations in New York, on October 2, 1975. Speaking in his bombastic style, he had emphasized, "We have to ensure UN Resolution 3379 passes today! Tell me why Palestine cannot gain National Status. This is their land!"

Dad had become the de facto Spokesperson for the Palestinian People and he did manage to successfully facilitate the passing of UN Resolution 3379 equating Zionism with Racism. However, nothing prepared him for the Hostage Saga popularly known as the "Entebbe Raid" which would occur nine months after the successful passing of UN Resolution 3379 and forever seal his fate in the age-old tussle between Abraham's children Ishmael and Isaac.

The "Raid" on Entebbe by Israelis

On the night of July 3, 1976 and the early morning of July 4, 1976, there was a "Raid" on Entebbe by the Israeli Elite Special Forces. They "raided" Entebbe to rescue fellow Israelis taken hostage by the Popular Front for the Liberation of Palestine (PFLP) on Air France Flight 139 at Entebbe Airport in Uganda. While this "Raid" was taking place, Dad was in Mauritius handing over the OAU (Organization of African Unity) Chairmanship to that country's leader. He had held the Chairmanship of the OAU from 1975 when the summit was held in Kampala, Uganda.

Sometimes referred to as "Operation Thunderbolt", the "Raid" has been dramatised in films such as Victory at Entebbe (1976) directed by Marvin J. Chomsky and Raid On Entebbe (1977) directed by Irvin Kershner, among others. Books on the "Raid" include William Stevenson's Ninety Minutes at Entebbe and Yoni's Last Battle: The Rescue at Entebbe by Iddo Netanyahu.

Additional information will be provided as the series Idi Amin: Hero or Villain? His Son Jaffar Amin and Other People Speak unfolds. However, Dad told us that he was actually supposed to be hijacked in a daring mid air operation by the

Israelis upon his intended return from Mauritius where he had gone to hand over the OAU (Organization of African Unity) Chairmanship. Upon being hijacked he was supposed to be escorted to Israel. However, Dad got wind of the event from General Lumago, a Kakwa who was Ambassador in Lesotho.

Apparently the Gulf Stream II (G II) that was given to him by the Saudi Royal Family in 1972 was ordered by him to take off almost vertically from Mauritius Airport at top speed, without leveling off then come down like a roller coaster ride to Entebbe Airport right away. This was to avoid Phantom Jets from either the Israeli or the American Aircraft Carriers. This is a highly technical outmaneuver few are familiar with but pilots do it to hasten flight time. Dad got home before the Israeli attack and he had already got to State House Entebbe when the attack started.

The likes of his pilots like Atiku, Abusala, Amunya and Kiiza of the Bunyoro Babito Royal Kingdom were Fighter Pilots trained in the USSR. When Pilots make scramble liftoffs from an airport being bombed or under attack, they normally do 60-45 degree liftoffs. They maintain that angle until they achieve maximum elevation (Altitude). Then they either level off or descend. Since the elevation between Seychelles and Uganda was sufficient to start descending towards Entebbe

Airport, in effect it looked like a Roller Coaster ride – up, then down and landing.

CHAPTER TEN

A "Conversation" with Major General Lumago

In a series titled Serving Amin that was published and posted online in Uganda's Newspaper the Sunday Monitor on June 5, 2005, Isaac Lumago talked to Tabu Butagira about the senior positions he held in Dad's administration. In the Article captioned "Foreign commanders let down Amin, says Maj. Gen. Lumago", Isaac Lumago confirmed that he had warned the Uganda Army of the impending "raid" on Entebbe. According to Isaac Lumago, at the rank of Colonel, Dad appointed him Minister of Industry and Power in 1975. Following is what he had to say in connection with the "raid":

"After putting things in the ministry right within four months, I was appointed an ambassador to Lesotho but accredited to seven other countries in southern Africa. This was in 1976".

"It was while in Lesotho that I informed the Ugandan army that Israelis were coming to raid the Old Entebbe Airport to rescue passengers, most of whom were Israeli, taken hostage by Palestinians aboard an Air France Boeing aircraft from Paris to Tel Aviv".

"I had undertaken extensive and high profile intelligence training with the Mossad in Israel,

CIA in America and the KGB in Russia. This is how I got the confidential information before hand that the Israelis were coming to raid Entebbe Airport to rescue their hostages".

In the Interview with Tabu Butagira, Isaac Lumago shared that army officials did not heed his warning about the impending "raid" by the Israeli Elite Special Forces.

"This was not our war. It was a fight between the Palestinians and the Israelis. As far as I was concerned, there was no need for our soldiers to get involved in it", offered Isaac Lumago. He clarified that he did not call to inform the Uganda Army so that they could fight the Israelis but he called them so that they could relocate the hostages away from the airport and prevent it from being destroyed.

Being "taunted" after the "Raid"

I was at Kabale Preparatory School in Kigezi District when the "Raid" occurred. Just as I came out of the outdoor bog house, Ian Bitwire, brother to Wilber Bitwire rushed up to me and asked me "What is your father's name?" I answered Idi Amin. "Another?" he prompted, I said Dada. "What else?" I said those are his names. Then Ian Bitwire started listing the titles "DSO, blah, blah, blah". Those are not names I blurted.

He started laughing while uttering "Bure Kazzi" ("Useless") then he pulled out the Newspaper footage showing a row of burnt Mig 21s and made the historical pronouncement of the Zionist "Operation Thunder" to me. Shocked and dreading the implications while a group gathered, ironically one Andrew Bemba the son of a Sergeant in the Uganda Army (UA) attending a Posh School no less…who had lost 20 soldiers during the "Raid", asked, "Was he killed?" With great anticipation from the assembled crowd, Ian answered "No", setting off regrets from the lot of them. "Aaaaaaaaaaaaaaaaah eeehyeeee!" they lamented in Bantu Fashion, about the fact that Dad hadn't been killed in the "Raid". They did this with regret.

That is when I released a weary smile and left them discussing the issue. Hahahahaha, hmmmmmmmmmmmm! I still laugh and muse in my head about Dad's ability to evade capture or murder.

A 180-degree turn and our Jewish siblings

I have often been asked for an opinion about Dad's 180-degree turn against Israel after being a loyal friend, strong supporter and ally for years and fathering twins with an Israeli Mossad Agent and following are some thoughts and reflections I have shared. I encourage readers to read thoughts and reflections by other people that will be included as background information for the section of the series titled "Other People Speak". However, as I explained in a previous section, Dad felt that since our Kakwa tribe was a tiny fraction of approximately 150,000 strong in a population of over 14 million at the time, it made political sense to cultivate additional constituencies within the Ummah (Community of Muslim Believers).

    In his opinion, there was no better way to pursue this agenda than to demonstrate unwavering and total support for Arab People who form the bulk of the Ummah. However, it was always interesting to watch the dynamics in my multi-religious family as members emphasized strong family ties over religious ties. This happens within the entire Kakwa tribe where numerous families are also multi-religious and they do not manifest the least bit of conflict because they belong to different religions – some even convert back and forth and partake in each other's celebrations. As an example, Grandma Aisha adored the people of Israel. She called them God's chosen people and her point of reference was the Bible because like Grandpa, Grandma was also a Christian before she converted to Islam and some ideas never leave your mindset.

    Regarding Dad's strong relationship with Israel before his 180-degree turn, we actually have

Jewish twin brothers born in 1971. If anything I believe Dad secretly lamented the split between himself and the Israelis because he had some lifelong friendships with individual Israelis but I guess the pursuit of a strong relationship with the Ummah precluded "double dealing" for Dad.

Dad always talked about how a lone Israeli Paratrooper skydived with a wreath with smoke trailing behind and laid it on Grandma's grave the time she died in 1969. This was when the relationship between Dad and the Israelis was still good - a most poignant salute by Colonel Balev to his friend Idi Amin's mother. It is ironic that Dad and Balev would "meet" again as antagonists and not friends under a brink man ship scenario during the Hostage Taking and "Raid" on Entebbe in 1976.

I have often reflected on my Jewish twin brothers fathered by Dad and sometimes wonder where they are. Then I guess that they are probably soldiers of some sort. Successful soldiers no less, since the mother is related to Moshe Dayan no less, and having a father like Idi Amin no less!

Whether people like it or not, Dad was an exemplary soldier – the best!

My siblings and I would definitely be open to the idea of trying to locate and meet our Jewish twin brothers by an Israeli mother as Dad used to show us letters our Jewish brothers wrote him every birthday from 1972, a year after they were born in 1971. The letters were accompanied with cherub twins smiling to the camera. Their mother dutifully sent these pictures to the twins' father my Dad.

The last word about our Jewish brothers came in 2008 from an Israeli expatriate who claimed that one of the twins joined his mother's profession as a Major in the Israeli Secret Service Mossad while his twin brother is also a Major in the Israeli Air Force. I have always fantasized about inviting my Jewish brothers to Uganda. It would be touching to invite them to Mount Liru, "the true place where the Jewish Prophet Moshe disappeared".

I have regularly reflected on my Jewish Siblings as well as my other siblings whom I have never met. I have dubbed these siblings "Falasha Twins" and "the Lost Boyz" respectively. Poignantly Annual Birthday celebration photos and letters kept streaming from the "Falasha Twins'" mother. However, they were sorrowfully first confined to Bomb and Poison Squad Letter Experts in the State Research Bureau, awaiting the all clear before they were sent to Dad's Permanent Secretary Balinda at the President's Office between 1971 and 1978 and the fall of their father from grace in 1979.

According to Shaban Abdul Tem, pictures and photographs in time of caramel coloured smiling twins facing the camera at various stages of growth were regularly sent to Dad between 1973 and 1978. God bless Nnalongo (mother of twins) for she kept sending the pictures and the children's letters to "Big Daddy" as Dad is often referred to by the time they were old enough to scratch out a few sentences to a father they would never know. Interestingly and simultaneously in Posh Schools strewn across the country, siblings of the twins I affectionately call Mikhael Adule Amin and Jibril Dombu Amin, went through the age long ritual of also writing letters to parents. They conveyed their thoughts and personal interests and usual childish requests. The Posh Schools strewn across the country that my siblings and I attended included such schools as Gayaza Primary School, Budo Primary School, St Mary's Namagunga Primary School, Namilyango Primary School and Kabale Preparatory School where I attended.

Hankering for the past after one of the lengthy revelations that characterized my conversations with Dad at our Al-Safa residence in Saudi Arabia in the 1980s, I once asked Dad where he thought my Jewish siblings were and he unexpectedly gave me a resounding rebuke. I liken his response to that of Muhammad Ali's response to the schism (parting of ways) between the Late Elijah Muhammed and the Late Malik El Shabaz (Shabab People's King) a.k.a. Malcolm X.

I was reliably informed in 2008 that one of my Jewish siblings followed his mother's profession into the secret services Mossad while the other followed his father's love affair with Aeronautics into the Israeli Air Force. They were apparently both at the rank of Major no less. Although the existence of these siblings is not common knowledge, Dad was fond of reminiscing about them to family members at both our former Makarona residence in Jeddah and at the Al-Safa residence in Jeddah near Souk Suriyah. That is where I got the gist to adlib into English the events as they unfolded.

Dad even told the tale to Israel's bitter enemies the Palestinians who were very close to the family in the nineteen eighties, at the height of the events surrounding Sharon's desecration of Lebanon and the horrific events at Shabra and Shatila refugee camps. Nevertheless they considered the fact that Dad was able to conceive with that "Proud Jewish Race" as Philosophical and Poetic Justice since they felt Dad was being used and manipulated in the past but he was the one who had the last laugh. I never liked to look at it from that politicized angle but felt a need at family level to get in touch with these Semitic siblings of mine and maybe introduce them to our highly misunderstood Nilo Hamitic (Plains Nilotic) Heritage.

CHAPTER TEN 143

A prayer for a Jewish-Muslim Peace Pact

I have taken up the task of gathering my siblings - the lost tribe of the Adibu Likamero Kakwa clan. Our oldest sibling Baba born in 1948, lives in Vancouver, Canada. A Somali brother born in Balet'uen in 1950 and a Somali Sister in Hargesia the same year are somewhere. Our lost Kikuyu Elders Njoroge and Njuguna born in 1951 and big brother Kazimoto born in 1952 all need to come into the Al-Amin family fold as Temezi (Elders) in order to complement the Official Heir and First Son Taban Idoru Amin who was born in 1958. Our brother Kazimoto prefers to live in Torit. We are truly a multinational family.

I ask my siblings wherever they might be to take time off and get in touch or pay a visit to their Paternal Homeland West Nile "The Heart Beat of Africa." They will be warmly welcomed and at the age of +38 years they are old enough to decide.

Whatever the misunderstanding between these two Nations in the past, I strongly believe that my grandmother's dying wish should be fulfilled through my Jewish twin brothers - the two Angels I have named Mikhael Adule Amin and Jibril Dombu Amin. This should happen as a fulfillment of a 21st century Jewish-Muslim Peace Pact between the children of Ishak and Ishmael (Isaac and Ismail) at a spiritual level. Let us keep

Armageddon at bay a little longer I pray Insha Allah (God Willing).

How Dad became entangled in the "Raid"

Dad felt the occasion was his chance to gain the spotlight on the world stage as a peacemaker. Alas! The world saw him as someone perilously pandering to the whims of terrorists! He lost 27 soldiers including the seven hostage takers.

Regarding the question who was responsible for "painting" Dad as someone perilously pandering to the whims of terrorists and what the reason/motivation was behind the "painting", the 1974 French Documentary on Dad titled, "General Idi Amin Dada: A Self Portrait" brought out a lot of issues. The Documentary was meant to explain Dad's views to the world. However, what comes across very strongly is his strong Anti-Zionist stance.

It is evident that the makers of the 1974 French Documentary turned the Documentary into an Anti-Zionist film instead of what Dad thought it was going to be – a broader explanation of his views to the world!

Thus the dye had been cast prophetically with hostages taking over an Airline he had jokingly suggested on silver screen during the making of the Documentary two years earlier in 1974!

Singing a "Gospel Song" for Dad

Dad once asked us to sing him a song so we lined up in front of him and belted out a Gospel Song. After we finished the song, he sat there stone-faced and the whole lot of us looked at each other expecting the usual clapping one gets at school only for him to lament:

"Muna yimba nyimbo la wa Kafir" ("You are singing the songs of unbelievers").

We all looked down in shame following the rebuke.

"Apana mbaya, he muzuri" ("This is not bad, it is good"), Dad tried to cheer us up with his favourite jest about his Christian family members.

"Wa kina Baba Siri'ba wana yimba kama nyinye" ("Those of Baba Siri'ba sing like you boys") Dad offered, referring to his Christian uncle Siri'ba and other Christian family members he held in high regard and had very close relationships with.

"Tuku Te Te Te Tendereza Yesuuuuuu", Dad imitated his Born Again Christian uncles and other Born Again Christian family members praising Jesus (Yesu) in a Luganda song sung by many Born Again Christians in Uganda, before finishing it with a volcanic shoulder-shaking laugh.

Luganda is the language of the Baganda tribe of Uganda and Dad and many of his family members spoke it fluently from living in Buganda.

My stepmother Mama Madina who was also Muslim born and bred had commented, "Ndiyo (Yes). They are singing Christian songs".

Following the rebuke by Dad for singing a Gospel Song, he got onto his "Air Phone" and called Mzee (Elder) Barnabas Kili, the Minister of Education and asked:

"Where can I get a Muslim teacher within Kabale? I do not want you to transfer someone. Get me a Primary School Teacher who is a Muslim and can teach my children Garaya (Qur'anic Studies/Readings) within Kabale Preparatory School. I do not want them teaching my children Sunday school. They will find time to practice our religion, do you hear me?"

Brigadier Barnabas Kili the Minister of Education found a Kiga by the name Zakaria. Unfortunately he would later claim in the book by Cameron titled, "The Rise and Fall of Idi Amin" that he was forced to come and teach the Idi Amin children against his will. Regardless of his future claims, Zakaria was a very good Geography teacher and even impressed the British missionaries who thought this was a ploy of Idi Amin's to introduce Islam to Kabale Preparatory School through the back door. However, the only children who were Muslims at the school were us, the children of Mzee Yusuf Odeke the CO (Commanding Officer) of Simba Battalion, an Acholi, Conrad Nkutu, who was known as Abdul Nkutu son of Shaban Nkutu and Minister Marjan's son who became a Medical Doctor. He arrived at the school in 1979 and was actually left there when Dad evacuated us during his impending fall in 1979.

The first thing we said when Dad sent a Platoon to rescue us during the war that led to his ouster was that we had left Yusuf Odeke's son Saidi Odeke and Marjan's 6 year old son behind. Dad was shocked but by the grace of God the missionaries looked after the boy and he went on to become a doctor. Every time I meet Marjan Jr. I repeat his favourite childish song "Kunene kookoo nene". He would also repeat that to the amusement of all.

Saidi Odeke was my classmate and managed to be vacated to the Congo after Dad's fall where he eventually linked up with his family.

In 2008 I was surprised to see a gentleman called Yusuf Odeke in the Kony Peace Talks (The Peace Talks between the Lord's Resistance Army and the Government of Uganda) contingent that came to Arua. I almost felt or sensed that it might be Saidi, for his father died in exile and I have always asked after Saidi Odeke. They were Acholi Muslims and his father was one of Dad's strongest

Dad's naughty jest on the British Royal Family

In 1977, Dad played a naughty but expensive jest on the British Royal Family and Secret Service. He "planned" to attend the Queen's Silver Jubilee in London with a troupe of 200 tribal dancers and then "decided" to "cancel" the trip.

He formally flew off from Entebbe International Airport having been seen off by his High Command and "swamped" by Reporters intended on writing about the fact that he was an unwelcome guest at the Queen's Silver Jubilee in London.

Unbeknownst to Reporters, the British Royal Family and Secret Service at the time, Dad took off in the G2 Presidential Jet that had been given by the Saudi Royal Family but headed for Gulu and Khartoum instead and then he returned to Entebbe. He was laughing hard as he did this – the same chesty laugh that accompanied a question posed to him by a French Reporter who compared him to Hitler on that boat ride at Kabarega Falls in the 1974 French Documentary on him titled, "General Idi Amin Dada: A Self Portrait."

According to Dad, his naughty but expensive jest set off a scramble by the British Secret Service to set up a fully armed response team that was supposed to counter the "danger" of his "imminent" and unwelcome arrival in London. Dad laughed hard because he had successfully "duped" Uganda's former colonial masters the British yet again and he thought this was very funny.

CHAPTER ELEVEN

The war between Uganda and Tanzania

Events relating to the war between Uganda and Tanzania that led to Dad's ouster on April 11, 1979 will be explored in more detail under the section of the series titled "Other People Speak". However, suffice it to say that relations between Dad and Julius Nyerere had continued to deteriorate, despite the time in 1973 when Dad extended an offer of the hand to Julius Nyerere at the 1973 OAU (Organization of African Unity) Summit in Addis Ababa, Ethiopia. At the time of the OAU Summit in Addis Ababa, Ethiopia in May 1973, Julius Nyerere and Dad had difficulties in their relationship and an ongoing conflict.

As outlined in previous sections, conflict had developed between Dad and Julius Nyerere immediately following the Military Coup that catapulted Dad to the position of President of Uganda on January 25, 1971 and Julius Nyerere granted Apollo Milton Obote political asylum in Tanzania.

In September 1972, Ugandan exiles had invaded Uganda through Tanzania and Dad felt that Julius Nyerere sanctioned the invasion. He considered it an act of aggression and declaration of enmity by Julius Nyerere.

Between September 1972 and October 1978, tensions had continued to build up between Dad and Julius Nyerere with the threat of war continuing to be imminent. Units of Dad's army were regularly placed on high alert in readiness for war and suspicion ran rampant. Most people in Uganda were always aware that as long as Dad was the President, it was just a matter of time before a full-blown war erupted between Uganda and Tanzania.

Stories and first hand accounts by Army Veterans and other individuals who were intimately involved in the ongoing conflict and the subsequent full-blown war between Uganda and Tanzania abound and they will be made available through the section of the series titled "Other People Speak". However, beginning in 1978, tension between Uganda and Tanzania increased with rumours of an impending attack on Uganda by Tanzania running wild! This led members of Dad's High Command to call for an immediate attack on Tanzania, which eventually happened in October 1978.

Before the attack, the Chui and Simba Battalions were rumoured to have mutinied over pay also in October 1978.

At this time, Dad made his biggest mistake and as it turns out, the final disastrous gamble by sanctioning the attack on Tanzania and occupying its territory - although on hindsight a close associate of his by the name Juma Oka was at the epicentre of this most unfortunate of blunders. He was nicknamed Butabika.

Juma Oka, nicknamed Butabika is the same Army Officer who put a gun to Dad's head back in 1971 when Dad became reluctant about taking over the Presidency following the Military Coup against Apollo Milton Obote on January 25, 1971.

Loyalty to his own forces led Dad to not openly clash with the invaders led by Juma Oka Butabika, although privately he was furious about the incident as he was ill informed about it when he sanctioned the attack!

According to reports, on October 27, 1978, sporadic border clashes and attacks ensued at the Border Town of Mutukula between the Uganda Army and the Tanzania People's Defence Forces. Then on October 31, 1978, the Uganda Army crossed into the Kagera Salient and attacked Tanzania. Juma Oka Butabika, one of Dad's officers, led the initial attack. He is reported to have phoned Dad and claimed that Tanzanian troops had invaded Uganda, which forced him to take charge of Ugandan soldiers stationed at the border areas in order to repel the Tanzanian invaders.

According to reports, Dad fell for the information given by Juma Oka Butabika and sanctioned more attacks on Tanzania.

After the attacks by Juma Oka Butabika, Dad went on air and declared "a world record" of twenty-five minutes in capturing some 700 square miles of Tanzanian territory. He announced that his government had annexed the Kagera salient.

Following the border clashes and attacks on Tanzania, there was widespread looting, rape, murder and destruction of unimaginable proportions in the Border Towns of Tanzania.

More details have now emerged about the circumstances surrounding the war between Uganda and Tanzania. These include allegations that Dad and his senior officers were given false and misleading reports by saboteurs and subversive elements operating within the State Research Bureau in order to start a war between Uganda and Tanzania so that Dad could be overthrown.

There are also allegations that others and not Dad or his senior officers orchestrated vicious atrocities on innocent civilians in Tanzania following the attack by Juma Oka Butabika which was sanctioned by Dad and made it look like Dad and his senior officers sanctioned these atrocities.

They allegedly did this so that Tanzania could be "pushed" to the limit and declare an all out war on Dad's government to defend itself and its citizens and to completely overthrow Dad.

In essence, the people making the allegations suggest that Dad, Juma Oka Butabika and Dad's other senior officers were duped into attacking Tanzania under false pretences and on false information that was given deliberately so that they could attack Tanzania and start a war. In addition, the same saboteurs and subversive elements allegedly went on to commit the most gruesome atrocities.

Some critics have boldly stated: "The widespread looting, murder and destruction in the Border Towns of Tanzania that followed the clashes between Tanzanian and Ugandan soldiers and the attacks by Uganda on Tanzania were committed by the same saboteurs and subversive elements that operated within Uganda and murdered innocent Ugandans throughout Idi Amin's rule. They did this to continue to tarnish Idi Amin's reputation and make him look like a maniacal murderer. They are cold hearted killers who were only interested in achieving their own agendas."

Needless to say, the horrific atrocities committed against innocent Tanzanian civilians provoked Julius Nyerere and his government to declare war on Dad. These atrocities indeed pushed Tanzania to the limit and necessitated the country's military to defend its innocent citizens against murders and other atrocities allegedly committed by others and not Dad's soldiers.

Moreover, powerful governments around the world had allegedly gone along with the propaganda that was ongoing against Dad and fully supported Tanzania and the exiles in their bid to overthrow Dad's government.

Allegations relating to the war between Uganda and Tanzania will be explored in more detail under the section of the series titled "Other People Speak" along with additional details on the war. However, in response to the "careless" "blunder" by Juma Oka Butabika, one of Dad's senior officers, soldiers comprising of Tanzanians, Ugandan exiles and mercenaries launched an attack on Mutukula.

They were determined to overthrow Dad's government and the Ugandan exiles were about to realize the objectives of the meeting they held in 1976 in Lusaka, Zambia to lay a more systematic strategy for overthrowing Dad. Uganda and Tanzania were now entangled in an all out war. The casualties would be many and the damages immeasurable!

Meanwhile, roughly 10,000-15,000 mainly young Uganda Army recruits passed out at Ngoma, northwest of Bombo and prepared to fight the guerrillas.

Having recently obtained armaments from the Soviet Union, Tanzania was more than prepared for the war against Dad and angry and determined enough to want to not only drive the so-called invaders out of Tanzanian territory but to completely overthrow Dad. So in November 1978, Tanzania launched a counter-attack on Uganda and on December 9, 1978, the country's President Julius Nyerere announced that the

CHAPTER ELEVEN

Tanzanian army had had a victory. He told Tanzanians that Dad's soldiers had been driven out of Tanzanian soil.

A Key Note: Actually, after the attack sanctioned by Dad and the announcement that his government had annexed the Kagera salient, nations from the OIC (Organization of the Islamic Conference) convinced him to withdraw back to the original borders that existed when each country achieved "Independence." Dad had done that but Tanzania attacked Uganda in retaliation nonetheless. Dad's soldiers were not driven from Tanzania as has been reported. They had withdrawn from the Kagera salient when Tanzania attacked Uganda.

According to another critic, "There was more to come as the Ugandan exiles seized the opportunity of the hostility that their members orchestrated between Tanzania and Uganda to implement their agenda to overthrow Idi Amin from power. The most gruesome atrocities committed by the exiles on innocent Tanzanians forced Julius Nyerere to jump on the exiles' bandwagon because the culprits made it look like the horrific atrocities were committed by Idi Amin's so-called invading army".

Stories and first hand accounts by individuals who were caught in the "crossfire" of the war between Uganda and Tanzania abound. They will be made available through the section of the series titled "Other People Speak", along with information relating to routes taken by the Liberators in Tanzania and Uganda.

An unnerving phone call to Dad about the war

I will never forget the time when my siblings and I were with Dad in the room as he took a call related to the hostility that was going on between Uganda and Tanzania. We were giving Dad the usual massage that day when he picked up the phone then slammed it down. He looked at me while I worked the sole of his 14-inch feet and said, "They have attacked me again…The Tanzanians. It is a big force this time".

After that momentous phone call and on our outing to Cape Town View Munyonyo, a long convoy of fancy cars brought the High Command up to the resort at "Cape Town View" in Kampala for a meeting with Dad. It was his style to have his children around him at his most trying of hours for he should have loaded us onto the Ubiquitous (Nissan Civillian) Omni Bus which used to transport the majority of his children to and from State House Entebbe. However, at this moment he kept us around.

Dad had the best Strike Force Protection Unit but having his children around him during times of war while on holiday seemed to be a comfort to him as is normal with any parent.

CHAPTER ELEVEN 159

There were rumors of a coup and the agenda from the delegation of high ranking officers was to ask him to step down.

Dad normally took us to Cape Town View Munyonyo during our school holidays and this was the last school holiday I spent with him before I joined Primary Six in 1979 at Kabale Preparatory School. It was a very tense time indeed and I realized that something was wrong because there were hordes of soldiers around whom I did not recognize - Bodyguards and Drivers of each individual Battalion and Brigade Commander. The High Command Council was trying to convince Dad to stand down and he said, "How can you ask me to do this?"

The situation worsened from then on and Dad relied on Non-Commissioned Officers and a sprinkling of Majors, Captains, others and his Crack Marines at Bugolobi, Moroto and the Uganda Air Force.

The death of Lieutenant Colonel Godwin Sule

After the confrontation with the High Command at Cape Town View Munyonyo, Dad's looming defeat was becoming obvious when suspicion around a so-called Friendly Fire was determined as the cause of death of the Valiant Christian Lieutenant Colonel Godwin Sule. He was one of the contingents of Anyanya troops who served the 2nd Republic of Uganda with diligence and care. After the so-called Friendly Fire incident, the regular soldiers lost morale yet on hindsight the Tanzania People's Defence Force invaders in 1979 had suffered a resounding setback at Rakai during what Sergeant Peter Andia a Keliko (Kaliko) from Jaki County Congo would have considered a Battle Royale. Sergeant Peter Andia joined the Uganda Army in 1966.

It was therefore a mystery for the then Chief of Staff to issue a "Part One Order" requesting all Battalions to withdraw 50 miles from Rakai into the swampy plains of Lukaya away from their resounding scene of victory. Normally an army would have consolidated their positions before retreating but they didn't, which lends credibility to allegations that Dad's army had been infiltrated by the enemy. Moreover coordinates given to the Air Force Pilots were "erroneously" targeting Uganda Army positions and not Tanzania People's Defence Force positions! The people behind this were allegedly found to be Lieutenant Colonel Yorecam and others.

Isaac Maliyamungu, Yusuf Gowa (Gowan), Lieutenant Colonel Yorecam, Brigadier General Taban Lupayi, a Sudanese Christian and a Muganda head of Military Logistics were accused of being bribed and alleged to have received fake dollars as part of a plot to defeat Dad's army from "within". It was alleged that the Logistics Personnel would "erroneously" reroute mortar shells to artillery gunners while artillery shells were sent to Battle Tank Position all in an effort to stall the war efforts and eventually defeat Dad.

It was alleged that Lieutenant Colonel Yorecam was found to be giving positions of the Uganda Army troops to the Uganda Air Force leading to consistent "Friendly Fire" on Uganda Army positions. This he allegedly did while also giving coordinates of Uganda Army troops to members of the Tanzania People's Defence Force who would continue to bomb the Uganda Army Troop Formations at the battle front.

African mysticism came to the fore when every time the Uganda Army soldiers changed Battle Formation they were met immediately with a barrage of BM21 Rocket fire, which was personally manned by one Major Boris of the USSR. The bullets were raining in like a scene from a Biblical hail and brimstones until they started believing a gun the soldiers dubbed "The "Saba Saba"" had a sophisticated roving eye, not realizing it was their very own Field Commander who was directly compromising them from within. When he was discovered with the very latest coordinates and the very next battle formation coordinates while radioing them out to the Tanzania People's Defence Force, his very troops waylaid him with lethal vengeance.

According to reliable sources, Brigadier General Taban Lupayi, a Sudanese Pojulu could have been implicated in the very same scheme for he put a lot of miles between himself and the war front together with Isaac Maliyamungu, a Zairian Kakwa when the 50 miles withdrawal took effect. The rot had truly set in!

The scene was set for the Uganda Army's last stand in the marshy plains of Lukaya where the so-called friendly fire that killed Godwin Sule occurred. With only 3 T55 Soviet Battle Tanks and a 106 Jeep, the rest of the Army had withdrawn or been hit on the battle field. The incompetent withdrawal or deliberate ploy to withdraw allowed the invading Tanzania Peoples' Defence Force to position, strengthen and consolidate their gains on the war front.

At the frontline waving at the Tanzanian Forces

As all this was going on, Dad did something only he could have done. He drove to the scene of Lieutenant Colonel Godwin Sule's death and actually waved at the Tanzania People's Defence Force Detachment that was fighting the Ugandan troops. The Detachment was a few meters away but instead of firing at Dad and killing him, they waved back in excitement like school children – the irony of an unnecessary war between Uganda and Tanzania! The Tanzanian troops clearly saw and knew that it was Dad waving at them but they did not shoot him!

After that incident, Dad had stormed into Nakasero Lodge that very night, in the Elevated Kangaroo Springed 200 E series Benz, which was a factory prepared rally car, with a string of "Five O Fours" in tow and the white Communication Land Rover at the rear. The vehicles were all covered - actually caked in camouflage river mud as a precaution against reflection. That day, Dad alighted with his usual tearful earthquake laugh. He was laughing at the spectacle of not being shot at by members of the Tanzania Peoples' Defence Force. He had alighted into the welcoming arms of the Nakasero-Kabale Preparatory School contingent that was now under the care of his favourite wife Sarah Kyolaba whom he married in 1975.

We were amused the next day to hear on the News that "Suicide Sarah" as my stepmother Sarah Kyolaba was referred to, had toured the Frontline with her husband Idi Amin. We rushed to her to confirm the news only for her to deny the News Item.

"I was here the whole night. That is your father on one of his pranks. He probably went with that new Musoga bride of his".

Dad married Mama Nnabirye, a Police Officer, Soldier and Presidential Escort in 1978. The incident that involved him driving to the Frontline and waving to the Tanzania Peoples' Defence

Forces occurred around the time there was the constant boom sound reverberating over Kampala in March 1979.

CHAPTER TWELVE

"Part One Order" to repatriate families

The die was cast when Lieutenant Colonel Sule was reportedly shot from behind while making a valiant defence of the marshy plains of Lukaya. The second damning Order from the Chief of the Defence Staff Major General Yusuf Gowa (nicknamed Gowan) of the Mijale Kakwa clan near the Aringa border in West Nile was for soldiers to repatriate their families to safety. Some claim it was a directive from Dad following the Cape Town View Munyonyo showdown during which his senior officers told him to step down. After Dad refused to step down, they allegedly said things like, "Let his Strike Force and Marines do the fighting if he does not want to step down".

This "Part One Order" dealt the last nail in the Uganda Army coffin because suddenly the most amazing logistical operation swung into action for all soldiers hailing from the West Nile District in Jaki County, the Congo in Kakwa County and Southern Sudan. There was total disarray in the whole rank and file of the Uganda Army because of its homogenous composition for truly speaking the Uganda Army was a complete composition of the whole country. They seemed to melt into the western, eastern northern hinterlands just like a scene from the Second Gulf War when 200,000 strong Republican Guards simply melted away into the hinterlands as the American Army attacked Baghdad.

That time, an estimated 36,000 to 40,000 Uganda Army soldiers melted away from the battle front leaving only the bombing sorties by the Air Force to keep the Tanzania Peoples' Defence Force at bay.

Amazingly, a reconciliation took place between Abiriga 99 whom Dad had discharged from the army and Dad and he was able to swing in his Aringa factions into a last ditch effort to defend Dad's regime. The whole High Command had dissipated for they must have "signed consent" to the request to ask Dad to step down and they must have duly given him the mutiny notice at that very extended Cape Town View meeting, leading to his blanket condemnation of all officers. Dad's High Command from Lieutenant Colonel right up to General was implicated in the request for him to step down.

Dad now relied on his Crack Marines and the Air Force while the rest of the Battalions went into irreversible implosion, with pockets from Moroto, Mbale and Abiriga 99's contingent from north western Bunyoro. By this time, Dad could only rely on a sprinkling of Majors and other senior officer ranks, Captains and Non-

Commissioned Officers to run the last ditch efforts to shore up his regime, which was in decline.

Dad only had the Iraqi trained Marines at his last hour although Taban Lupayi had removed most of his Sudanese contingent during the infamous 50 miles withdrawal. It looked like only the 15,000 new recruits who were passed out just when the Kagera war started in 1978 were being deployed to the war front. The rest were in disarray.

The resounding factor that keeps replaying in all strong men regimes is the high propensity to have a "Republican Guard"-like Brigade that owes allegiance to the ruler. This recurrent theme in most "Third World" countries played into the familiar process of defeat just like what happened a decade later with the DSP in Mobutu's Zaire and then the Republican Guards in Saddam Hussein's Iraq. Quite often, grudges come to the fore at the final hour of defeat and quite often the regular soldiers leave the so-called Elite to "face the music". It was recalled by many how the regulars would say, "Let his Marines and Strike Force fight his battle for they always got the best from the rest." Grudges came to the fore during that time.

The last standing command centre comprised of Major Muhammed Luka Yuma of the Strike Force Presidential Guards, Major Mzee Yosa with Operations Intelligence Services, State Research Bureau, Captain Asio with State House

Signals, 3 T55 Soviet Battle Tanks Marine and 1 "one zero six" Jeep at Malire.

The rot started with the dismissals of key Aringas who owed their loyalty to the Vice President by tribal affiliation and it continued after Dad's ouster including incidents that occurred during a future "war" between the Kakwa tribe and the Aringa tribe in October 1980.

Allegations that Dad's army had been bought off

There was talk of the entire Uganda Army High Command from the Generals right down to the Majors having been bought off with fake US dollars to stall the defense efforts of the Uganda Army. Dad was aware of this and he was increasingly relying on the Junior Officers and his Crack Striking Force Bodyguards under Major Luka's Command.

Dad's last stand in 1979 was that undertaken by the valiant Lieutenant Colonel Godwin Sule of the Paratroopers School Malire who died in the "frontline" at Lukaya, fighting the combined Tanzania Peoples' Defence Forces and Ugandan guerrillas. Henceforth, the battle swung in favour of the guerrillas and the Tanzania Peoples' Defence Forces.

On March 19, 1979, following Lukaya and Lieutenant Colonel Godwin's death resulting from a so-called "Friendly Fire", Dad seemed to have been discouraged and presumed to have disappeared into a world of fantasy with those bombastic propaganda statements of his on Uganda Broadcasting Corporation (Radio Uganda). The state controlled Radio Station reported that Dad was visiting Mbarara for top-level strategic discussions with the officers of the Simba (Lion) and Chui (Leopard) Battalions.

Our rescue by a Platoon

Caught up in the momentous "surge" were a bunch of pre-teenage children of the man the Liberators wanted to topple – my siblings and I!

As it turned out, Mbarara had been in enemy hands for almost a month and the two units mentioned above had ceased to exist as organized forces. Although on hind sight, the announcement somehow or other coincided with a personal mission to rescue his loved ones from Kigezi District – my siblings and I.

Dad sent a King Air Turbo Propeller Plane to pick us up after we were rescued from our Boarding School in Kigezi District by a Platoon he sent and a lengthy stay at Hotel Marguerita. I believe it was during our stay at Hotel Marguerita that Dad needed to give the impression that Mbarara was still under the control of his government and the two Uganda Army units were still in existence. He needed to maintain that façade until he had sent the Plane that transported us to safety from our lengthy stay at the Hotel Marguerite.

We always knew Dad loved and cared for us very deeply. However the length to which he went to organize a daring rescue to get my siblings and I out of harm's way from the war zone could not have been a truer testimony of that love!

In 1979, while the war between Uganda and Tanzania was heating up, Dad sent an Army Platoon to rescue my siblings and I from being cut off by forces determined to overthrow his regime. This happened while we were still studying in Boarding School in Kabale in Kigezi District.

My siblings and I were sent to the elite missionary schools such as Kabale Preparatory School in Kigezi District for the boys and St. Mary's Namagunga for the girls. Dad felt good that we could attend the elite schools to which he had once been denied access because his family was erroneously considered Sudanese and "outsiders". Because they were not considered Ugandans, Dad was denied formal education. That was why he only attempted Primary School up to Primary IV, which was the limit set by the Colonial Administration for Muslims. He sporadically combined this attempt with Garaya (School of Qur'anic Studies/Readings). This had happened from the year 1940 when he was 12 years old to the year 1944 when he was 16 years old.

Al-Qadhafi Garrison Primary School, one of the schools my siblings and I went to was close to an armory and the site of a confrontation between troops loyal to my father and the opposition in June-July 1971. Everyone was in the dormitory under big metal beds with gunfire raging outside. It was unbelievable for a small kid. Our guardian eventually came in and told us everything was fine. The people trying to attack had been forced back.

After that confrontation between Dad's forces and the opposition, we were transferred to another barracks. I suppose you could say our father had put us in danger, but he always had key people to look after his affairs. He made sure we had Guardian Angels. So when it became evident that my brothers and I would be cut off by the troops that overthrew him in 1979, Dad did everything possible to rescue us.

Sergeant Tirikwendera a Munyamulenga from Goma in my Dad's Crack Presidential Guards, ominously pestered Dad to rescue us his children. We were about to be cut off in the Kigezi District in 1979 when the Liberation Forces were making their rapid push for Masaka and Ankole District during their lightning advance towards Uganda's Capital Kampala. Dad had initially thought that we would be safe in the care of the missionaries. However, Sergeant Tirikwendera insisted that the Hima/Tutsi grapevine was giving ominous signs that "Amin's children at Kabale Preparatory School would be targeted for destruction". Eventually, Dad gave up and put Sergeant Tirikwendera in charge of a Platoon that set off in a Brilliant (convict) Orange 4X4 All Terrain Military Bus (Fiat 75) towards Kabale, passing Masaka and Ankole just before the Tanzanian Army took over the Area.

Previously we had unexpectedly started to receive Military Police Guards from Baba Rajab (Captain Rajab of the Kakwa ethnic group) every evening that guarded each and every one of the three dormitories that we resided in at Kabale Preparatory School. When the missionaries asked us to inquire why the military were being posted outside every dormitory, the soldiers simply stated that they had orders to guard the President's children.

That eventful night, Miss Samna from Mersey side who was the Resident Matron at "The Warren" dormitory where I resided woke us up deep in the night informing us to dress quickly and prepare to leave. I did not know why and was surprised that we were leaving for home just shortly after the Half Term of my 1st term PLE in P6 of February 1979. We were not required as it were to take anything and I remember eyeing my chocolate brown Haji Kadingidi Platforms, checkered beige Bell Bottoms and chocolate brown Polo

CHAPTER TWELVE

neck top with longing when we were forced to leave everything behind.

I only got a very last glimpse of my beloved Miss Mary Hayward just as we climbed into the Orange Fiat 75. I was struck by the multitude of weaponry inside the All Terrain Bus and the stern attention from the Platoon sent to rescue us. They were Dad's Presidential Strike Force Guards.

To us children and to my mind in particular this was straight out of the Famous Five series. As the powerful bus set off, I even asked Sergeant Tirikwendera why we were not heading towards Mbarara when he turned towards Kisoro having descended down Rugarama Hill and just past my classmate Ezekiel's house. He solemnly told me that part of the country had been cut off by the invading Tanzanian Army.

We trudged through Wakaraba valley towards Kisoro. Mbarara was now in enemy hands and the two Uganda Army units there had ceased to exist as an organized force in the area. We would have to head for Kisoro, pass into Rwanda, cross over into Zaire (Congo) and then back into Uganda around Lake George and Lake Edward through the Queen Elizabeth National Park in order to escape the invading Tanzanian Army. We would then go to the Hotel Marguerite where we would wait for a plane Dad was sending to fly us to Entebbe.

I remember the tremendously steep descent enroute around the Kisoro area. The soldiers later told me that we were lucky witnessing the location deep in the night because the abyss was not a sight for the faint hearted. What an amazing trek!

This will always stick in my mind's eye. We only had a Military Police backup from the Kabale Barracks who escorted us in a Military Land Rover. Just as we entered the National Park deep in the night, somehow one of the sockets to the battery power came off and the powerful bus ground to a halt right in the middle of the National Park. The Military Police tried to alight and fix the problem but they were very alarmed by the slowly advancing laughter from hyenas in the area, which seemed to be daring the soldiers to try their luck! Anyone who has ever heard the sound of a hyena's laugh will know what I am talking about. The Captain Officer in Charge then decided that we would have to rest in the car until early morning the next day.

At dawn, Sergeant Tirikwendera, probably a veteran Truck Driver alighted and simply re-plugged the battery and the powerful machine kick-started instantly. We set off on a speedy romp through the park but came to a mile long traffic jam of heavy goods trucks — trucks that had got stuck in metre deep ditches. I will always remember the initial bemused looks on the hardened Truck Driver's faces when Sergeant Tirikwendera made a detour on the side of the stranded trucks, then amazingly managed to pass the multitude of trucks to the grudgingly respectful stares of the Truck Drivers.

The drivers longingly looked on as we effortlessly trudged forwards in that brilliantly orange All Terrain Military Bus. We came out near the Kazinga Channel, a conduit that links Lake George to Lake Edward. We were able to join the tarmac road right up to Hotel Marguerita at the foothill of Mountain Rwenzori, inside Queen Elizabeth II National Park.

Dad sent a King Air Turbo Propeller Plane to pick us up after a lengthy stay at this memorable hotel that bears my mother's name. While residing at Hotel Marguerita, the Officer in Charge of Kabale Military Police Barracks one Captain Rajab Rembi, a former Uganda Cranes no 11 winger in the 1960s tentatively managed to teach a gangly flat footed laid back 12-year old how to play pool in the Bar room area. I still remember the lessons I received from Captain Rajab. l also remember the misty atmosphere one sees at the foot of Mount Rwenzori. What a beautiful sight! Dad later shocked us when he claimed that there was an attempt by the advancing Liberation Forces to shoot down the plane with Anti-Aircraft Fire as it approached the Mpigi Area.

Other than the turbulence experienced around the lakeshores as the King Air Plane approached Entebbe Airport, nothing much happened apart from my sister Asha Aate Mbabazi tagging my sweater and owning up that she had wet herself. I placed my 6-year old sister to the side and indeed my "Idi Best" ("Sunday Best") trousers were all wet. Upon arrival, I rushed to the Children's Wing to change, while she was rushed to her mother Mama Mary's. At the time, Mama Mary was the Private Secretary for Social Affairs at the President's Office.

Our last days in Uganda

Upon arriving in Kampala, we were tentatively placed at Buganda Road Primary School by the Chief Presidential Protocol Nasr Ondoga who was responsible for all the President's personal affairs, for the final duration of our childhood stay in our beloved country. All the children who had left Kabale (apart from Mwanga Alemi and Asha Mbabazi) went to reside with Mama Sarah Kyolaba at the present day Kampala State House Nakasero (formerly Nakasero Lodge). Mwanga Alemi went to reside with his mother at Command Post Kololo and Asha Mbabazi went to reside with her mother also in Kololo.

During this time, no one was residing at Entebbe State House and it was only used for State Functions as Entebbe was near the war front and constant infiltration from the porous "Masaka,

CHAPTER TWELVE

Mpigi Coastline" rendered it unsafe to stay in. This was mostly in March 1979 and Kampala was taken in April 1979.

Dad's bombastic propaganda statements continued on radio. On March 26, 1979 the Uganda Broadcasting Corporation (Radio Uganda) announced that the President was "cut off at Entebbe." We would go so much as to affirm Dad's victory announced by the Uganda Broadcasting Corporation on March 26, 1979 when it announced that "the President was "cut off at Entebbe" but managed to repel the enemy forces with the support of loyal troops". The announcement by the Radio Station might have had some truth in it since this was the exact time Dad was negotiating with Al-Qadhafi to receive his immediate family into Tripoli and he needed the still useful Entebbe International Airport. The invading troops were still more than 70 miles away from Kampala when Dad was negotiating with Al-Qadhafi to receive us. Since vanguards of the so-called Liberation Forces had possibly already infiltrated some parts of the route to Entebbe by the time Dad was frantically trying to get us out of Uganda, he addressed the nation during which he asked "Ugandans who believe in God to pray day and night."

The Liberators intensified their efforts because they were hell bent on overthrowing Dad. On March 27, 1979, the "Liberation bombs" commonly referred to by Indigenous Ugandans as "Saba-Saba", landed on the compounds of the Republic House at Mengo and the Army Shop nearby in the evening. Meanwhile, a cabinet in waiting had been formed by The Uganda National Liberation Front (UNLF) in Moshi on March 24 and 25, 1979. This cabinet had been formed out of 22 political groups that had emerged in opposition to Dad's regime. Details about these groups and the formation of the cabinet are contained in a subsequent part of the series titled "The Liberators' Dysfunctional Alliances".

On March 28, 1979, about 9:00am, Lieutenant Colonel Pangarasio Onek, CO (Commanding Officer) of General Headquarters, Mbuya, instructed his troops to ambush any available means of communication: matatus, trucks, tractors, cars, taxis, etceteras, to take their families "home." My Avatar Yuga Juma Onziga knew there and then that it was "a game over" for Dad's regime. Dad's Army was in total disarray and it was now fighting to "save their skins."

The war ended at Lukaya when most of the soldiers and Secret Service Personnel either said "Congo na gawa" or "Sudan na gawa" and hightailed it out of the country. Some even said let him fight this out with his favourite Air Force and Marines – a reminder of the dangers of favoring particular units in the military over others.

CHAPTER TWELVE

As Dad's Army continued to disintegrate, his bombastic propaganda statements continued on state controlled radio but by now Dad knew better. On March 28, 1979, the Uganda Broadcasting Corporation (Radio Uganda) claimed that Dad had "smashed through the Tanzanian forces and reopened the road to Entebbe" from it being closed by the Liberators. The Uganda Broadcasting Corporation (Radio Uganda) and Dad may have been living in a dream world as the world would have wished it to be but privately Dad knew better. The bluff and the bombast that had served him well for eight years were rapidly losing their effect. As a consolation, Dad was now fighting a private war to evacuate some eighty members of his family and close associates to safety in Libya. Meanwhile the District Commissioner of Kampala, Muhammad, addressed a rally in Kampala and he urged people to turn for work and business as usual, yet the rebels were actually 20 miles outside Entebbe at the time.

On March 28, 1979 at about 4:00 pm, my Avatar Yuga Juma Onziga along with his wife and a two-week old baby girl, his father and brother, fled to Arua. But, at between Kiryadongo Hospital and Karuma Falls, the car, a Toyota matatu, they rented overturned and some people were injured but none seriously. The matatu was totally written off and Juma lost his JVC radio and stereo cassette in this accident.

Fortunately, his younger brother, who was driving later from Kampala also to Arua, stopped by and conveyed his wife and child along to Arua. The rest of them transferred to a nearby lorry and arrived in Arua early in the morning of March 29. They finally converged at their clan village of Rugbuza later that afternoon. The rest is history!

The same day March 28, 1979, Tanzanian long-range artillery began bombing Kampala. At about 11:20 pm, the Uganda Broadcasting Corporation broadcasted a news flash saying the attack was close by. "Tonight ... is the first time when the Tanzanian aggressors with mercenaries and traitors, using long-range artillery, have bombarded Kampala..." a newscaster announced. This admission of truth by the Uganda Broadcasting Corporation made Ugandans realize how close Dad's fall was.

At that time the truth about Dad's impending downfall remained concealed by the Kampala authorities. However, BBC World Service regularly intercepted Radio Uganda broadcasts from their monitoring station at Caversham Park in England. Ugandans who were brave and bold enough to follow the events at the risk of being discovered by the notorious State Research Bureau intelligence agents continued to quietly keep track of BBC broadcasts and the truth about Dad's impending defeat. They had begun to do so early in the war.

CHAPTER TWELVE

I will never forget the last days of our stay in Uganda due to the constant boom sound made by the "Saba-Saba BM21", the Artillery and BM 21 rocket shellfire into the Capital Kampala by the Liberators. Having been picked up from Dad's residence in Nakasero where we were residing at the time, we were all gathered at Command Post, another residence of Dad's. Then we set off in a convoy towards Munyonyo (Cape Town View) and used the Garuga detour towards Entebbe, coming out near Kajansi since some Liberation troops had already cut off and probably laid an ambush on the Main Road probably around the Lubowa Estates Area. We arrived at the old colonial residences (State House Entebbe), to await the planned flight to Tripoli, Libya.

Mama Sara Kyolaba had preferred to stay at Nakasero Lodge in Kampala even though she and Dad's wife Mama Madina previously jointly shifted to State House Entebbe, which has a better defense position following attempts to raid the Kampala residences by insurgents. In 1978, Mama Madina had left to go to Iraq together with Mama Nnabirye the Presidential Bodyguard Dad married during the same year 1978. Mama Nnabirye was in residence at the Cape Town View Resort before leaving to go to Iraq with Mama Madina.

Mama Madina had a detached retina while the expectant bride Mama Nnabirye went for precautionary tests. After the fall of Dad's government, the two women ended up first in Central Africa then in Paris, France after the fall of Bokassa, President of the Central African Republic and Dad's friend, also in 1979. My sister Zamzam Mama Nnabirye's daughter was born in Bangui the capital of the Central African Republic on the night of the Military Coup against Bokassa. Then she and Mama Madina left together for Mobutu's Kinshasa in 1979 via Paris, France where Catherine Bokassa had taken refuge.

CHAPTER THIRTEEN

The day my family fled to Libya in a Cargo Plane

The day my family fled to Libya we could hear the artillery shells in the distance getting closer. It was amazing and there was a sense of disbelief. This huge convoy set out from Kampala to Entebbe Airport. Dad was having 60 to 80 seats installed in a Cargo Plane for all of us. He was talking to Al-Qadhafi on the phone, telling him, "My children are coming". Dad sent us ahead but he wanted to stay on to make his last stand, even though he knew that the war was lost.

Apparently, a reluctant Egyptian pilot had to be commandeered and he was paid cash down in hard currency so that he could accept to fly the President's children out of the country to safety. The bombardment was only 20 miles away then. The Boeing 707 Cargo Plane had recently come in from one of its expensive cargo transport flight of coffee to the USA and he (The Pilot) was very tired. It had no seats whatsoever. So, some sixty to eighty seats were hurriedly placed in the plane to accommodate probably sixty persons who were given blankets against the cold emanating from the bare aluminum floor. I had actually been hurriedly discharged from Mulago Hospital following a sprain of my ankle and still had an itchy plaster of Paris on.

The Boeing 707 managed to take off under strange circumstances, due to the fact that artillery shellfire was now raining into the airport area. The Bodyguards were forced to place four cars around the plane and they raced down the runway as lighting for the pilot until we were airborne!

What an uncomfortable ride to safety this was, all the way to Tripoli! The plane ride to Tripoli, Libya was rough and uncomfortable. I have often reflected about what could have gone wrong with a plane that had no seats and was flown by a reluctant Egyptian pilot that had to be commandeered and paid in hard currency, before accepting to fly the President's children out of the country to safety. I have often wondered what would have happened if the Egyptian Pilot didn't honour the hefty bribe he received from Dad to fly us out of Uganda to safety but decided not to dwell on the predicament. Some say it was the fatigue that built the reluctance and no civilian pilot wants to work under a war situation, which was understandable under the circumstances.

We left behind some very prized items. I still see in my mind's eye an ornate golden Mantle Clock left in my Dad's state bedroom that was given to Dad by Tito of Yugoslavia on one of his last state visits to the Balkans. That visit holds a lot of meaning to me since Dad had promised me that if my grades improved he would take me on his next visit abroad. My grades did improve but my brother Lumumba was chosen on that particular trip and I remember my kid brother feeding a giraffe in the Belgrade Zoo on a photo shoot with the World War II hero. I remember asking my stepmother Mama Sarah if she had remembered to bring the Mantle Clock and she regretted that alas it had stayed in State House Entebbe.

The time Dad's Presidential Guards waylaid him

Mzee Yosa and Sergeant 'Bhuga played an exemplary role in getting Dad out of harm's way. For all the allegations of cowardice and other characterizations leveled against Dad over the years by his foes, at the 11th hour, Dad proved all these allegations and characterizations wrong. Here was a man true to character of the old colonial Kings African Rifles, who against the advice of his officers and Crack Presidential Guards had decided to remain in Kampala to await his fate after having ensured that his loved ones had been evacuated. "A Captain does not abandon his ship" scenario was played out to devastating effect on April 6, 1979 when Dad made an announcement on radio that he would stay in Uganda.

Dad made a final broadcast in Kampala on Uganda Broadcasting Corporation. During this broadcast he called Ugandans not to be afraid of the "cowardly enemy bombardment with a long range Artillery", adding that "the enemy has only seized part of South Buganda, together with a little part of Ankole." Dad insisted, "I will stay here except when I leave Kampala for another place in Uganda". This announcement by Dad prompted Senior Army Officers Mzee Yosa, Sergeant 'Bhuga from the Gimara Kakwa clan, Captain Asio of the Nyooke Kakwa clan and several hefty Presidential Guards to waylay their Commander-in-Chief and restrain him. They actually immobilized him in the process with straps and placed him in his factory prepared 200 series Mercedes Benz copue Rally car. On April 11, 1979 when his government was overthrown, Dad was still at Munyonyo in the vicinity of Kampala. He wanted to die in battle like a true soldier but several of his Presidential Guards would not let him. Then the convoy of Expensive Flagship Mercedes Benz 240 SEL 6.4s set off in tow for Jinja just as Kampala was overwhelmed by the Liberators. Major Mzee Yosa and Sergeant 'Bhuga and Captain Asio played an exemplary role in getting Dad out of harm's way.

Dad's last emotional speech

At Jinja, Dad made an emotional speech to Ugandans in general and the Basoga in particular as he was fleeing to safety in a convoy headed for

Arua and Ko'boko in Northern Uganda. He had stopped over in Jinja, Busoga when he addressed Ugandans through an assembled crowd of Basoga. He actually spent one week in Jinja while the Uganda National Liberation Front, the exiled group that overthrew his government through Tanzania consolidated their hold on Kampala.

While Dad was still at Jinja, he announced that this was where he would stand and die. He made the Ad-hoc speech in front of the Basoga reminding them and his country men of all the goodness he had tried to do for his fellow native Africans and yet "all the thanks he gets for it is them turning against him". He made an impassioned reminder to them to recall how they would even curiously heft up several flocks of livestock at will to where they resided without anyone disturbing their peace. Some of the people would even heft their livestock up to their high-rise apartments and no one would stop them. "You want me to go but one day you will lament that maybe I was good for the country after all." "You will then look for me but you will not find me". "People will cry after me but they will not find me" Dad continued, amidst the initial murmurs of "Agende Kajambiya".

Ironically, Dad's address to Ugandans through an assembled crowd of Basoga is the same speech Ugandans lament over decades later after witnessing years of grinding poverty and seeing the truth come to pass in that singular farewell. According to him, he spent the one week post April 11, 1979 the day of his total defeat and overthrow with Jumba Masagazi between Jinja and the Malaba-Busia Border trying to release the fuel his regime had paid for but they claimed that a new government was in place.

On Wednesday April 11, 1979 at 7:00 am, deposed Dad advised his troops on Radio Deutsche Welle in the Federal Republic of West Germany:

"Mimi badu Rahisi ya Uganda. Usi tupa bunduki yaku. Kufa na bunduki yaku" ("I am still the President of Uganda. Don't throw away your gun. Die with your gun"). That was the first time many people (including my Avatar Juma) heard him speak after his final broadcast in Kampala.

The fall of Kampala and celebrations

On Wednesday, April 11, 1979, the BBC World Service announced the fall of Kampala to the Tanzanian forces commanded by Colonel Benjamin Msuya. BBC correspondent John Osman and BBC stringer Charles Harrison had kept the world abreast with the rapidly changing military situation in Uganda. Late on April 10, 1979, unconfirmed reports had said the Tanzanian forces were already in Kampala. John Osman the BBC Correspondent had interviewed Dad in February

1977 on the circumstances of the deaths of Anglican Archbishop Janan Luwum and two cabinet ministers Lieutenant Colonel Wilson Erinayo Oryema and Charles Oboth-Ofumbi. So he had closely followed events that unfolded in Uganda that preceded Dad's "speedy" fall from the "highest position in the land" and he was familiar with Uganda's politics. However, Radio Uganda was silent on the news. Instead the home service on medium wave and the external service on short wave frequencies were both playing light music between transmission intervals.

Then at about 3:56 pm on April 11, 1979, transmission on Uganda Broadcasting Corporation (Radio Uganda) was interrupted. After a few moments of silence, the heavy Luo-accented voice of a man came on air. He introduced himself as Lieutenant Colonel David Oyite-Ojok. In a broadcast that was not very clear, the words "...Idi Amin is no longer in power..." filtered through. At 4:20 pm that afternoon, Lieutenant Colonel Oyite-Ojok's announcement was repeated on the home service of Radio Uganda. This was the historic message broadcast on that fateful day by David Oyite-Ojok:

"Fellow countrymen, I am Lieutenant Colonel David Oyite-Ojok. On behalf of the Uganda National Liberation Forces, I bring you good news. The Ugandan Liberation Forces have captured the Uganda...capital of Kampala today

Wednesday, 11 April 1979...Idi Amin is no longer in power..."

However, something odd happened at 5:00 pm when the external frequency of Uganda Broadcasting Corporation (Radio Uganda) came on air on short wave, out of the blue, playing light music. Those old enough to remember would know that the external service of Radio Uganda broadcasted from the Dakabela relay station in Soroti, 208 km east of Kampala. Then it went off air as abruptly as it had come on.

"What was going on?" asked nervous Ugandans. There was silence for more than four hours, which only heightened the tension in Kampala. Then at 8:00 pm, the state owned radio in Dar-es-Salaam, Tanzania announced in Kiswahili that it was now going to link up with Radio Uganda in Kampala for a special message. Then in English, came the announcement, "This is Radio Uganda. Stand by for an address to the nation by Mr. Yusuf K. Lule, Chairman of the Executive Committee of the Uganda National Liberation Front." During that broadcast, it was formally announced that Yusuf Lule had become the new president of the Republic of Uganda. A provisional government was announced and Ugandans were told that elections would be held "as soon as possible."

Significantly, Uganda's radio station had called itself "Radio Uganda" rather than "Uganda

Broadcasting Corporation" as it was known in Dad's era. As the then BBC Nairobi Editor for monitoring, Tom Heaton recalls, "This gave us a clue as to what to watch out for on the Soroti external frequency." At 10:00 O'clock the same night, the home service of Radio Uganda closed down but 35 minutes later, the external service short wave frequency broadcasting from Soroti suddenly announced, "Dear listeners, this is the external service of Uganda Broadcasting Corporation..."

At 10:41 pm, there came another segment of broadcasting. There were two voices - one male and unknown, the other, a low soft Baritone bass familiar to Ugandans, the international community and especially weary diplomats for eight long years. That voice was Dad's and the broadcast segment went like this: Voice one: "Hello!" Voice two: "Are you ready?" Voice one: "Yes, we are ready, please, Your Excellency." Then voice two again: "I, President Idi Amin Dada of the Republic of Uganda, I would like to denounce the announcement made by Lieutenant Colonel Oyite-Ojok, the so-called Chief of Staff, that my government has been overthrown and they have formed their rebellion government in Uganda..."

It was now clear that Dad was in Soroti, broadcasting on his sophisticated electronic equipment that he had frequently used on his upcountry tours. Dad gave a second version of his speech from Soroti in Kiswahili but it was the largely ineffective defiance of a desperate leader, now deposed.

Unbeknown to most Ugandans, there were three individuals who had particular vested interests in events that were unfolding in Uganda at the time Dad was overthrown. These three people followed broadcasts on Radio Uganda with intense interest. Listening to Radio Uganda from Jinja but utilizing his wireless communication facility was Dad, the 51-year old now deposed President of Uganda while the 54-year old former President of Uganda Apollo Milton Obote was also intently listening in Dar-es-Salaam, to developments in Kampala. This was happening as Uganda's new Minister of State for Defence, 35-year old Yoweri Kaguta Museveni was listening to developments live on Radio Uganda in Kampala as he actively helped to secure the captured city Kampala, in dark green battle fatigue.

The first scene of Rembi's Mystical Legacy on January 25, 1971 to April 11, 1979 was finished. The second scene was 13 months away and it would happen in Bushenyi on May 27, 1980 when Apollo Milton Obote alighted and Pope-like kissed mother Earth as he stepped on Ugandan soil again. The third scene was to wait for February 6, 1981 at Kabamba Barracks. It was to strike Liberation Politics when a disgruntled politician cum Freedom Fighter Yoweri Kaguta Museveni,

CHAPTER THIRTEEN

along with an overwhelmingly Tutsi fighting force decided that the barrel of the gun was the only option for the ultimate route to power. Whether he should have given the chair to the rightful winner of Uganda's first elections after Dad was deposed, Democratic Party boss Semogerere was besides the point in the "Roots of Treason". The "Roots of Treason" is what I have titled my explanation of the "Domino Effect" and the anarchy that occurred when the power vacuum enveloped Uganda after Dad's fall from grace which I outline in my book titled "Rembi's Mystical Legacy."

On April 11, 1979, Dad was toppled and there was a Cabinet in waiting ready to take over the Uganda Government. However, President Yusuf K. Lule ignored the list compiled by Apollo Milton Obote at Julius Nyerere's request and hastily named a cabinet of his own, which would lead to his speedy downfall and set off a multitude of coups that characterized an unprecedented dysfunction in Ugandan Politics.

On the day Dad was toppled, there were "celebrations", "celebrations" and more "celebrations" reminiscent of the ones that occurred when he took over power from Apollo Milton Obote in 1971. There were also rampant killings of people labeled as Dad's henchmen - the sometimes-unfair reference to anybody associated to Dad by tribe, religion and region of origin, including people who did not benefit from his rule in Uganda.

These scenes replayed themselves over and over again.

On Wednesday, April 11, 1979 when his government was overthrown, Dad was still at Munyonyo in the vicinity of Kampala. He wanted to die in battle, like a true Soldier but several of his Presidential Guards would not let him.

Dad running the gauntlet on the way to safety

On April 22, 1979, when Dad passed through Lira and Gulu in Northern Uganda, he was still intended on hanging on to power. However it was only a distant dream at this time. Nonetheless, he continued his feeble attempts to hang onto power.

On April 13, 1979, while still broadcasting from the relay station in Soroti in Teso District and later still, on the Gilgili Radio Station at Arua probably on a recorded tape, Dad was still telling Ugandans that he was their President. However, deep down, he knew that he had been done in.

One of Dad's associates and entourage Mzee (Elder) Kivumbi was able to give a blow by blow account of their movements between April 10, 1979 and April 23, 1979 when they arrived in Arua. According to reports, there were incidents of them running the gauntlet between heavy fighting in Teso, trees being cut onto the roads in Lan'go land to block Dad's convoy from passing through and an incident in Gulu. The so-called Luo Militias had risen up, realizing that the Nation had changed hands but Dad passed through all hostile territory without being hurt and experiencing some of the fiction included in the book and film about him titled "Rise and Fall of Idi Amin".

A harrowing incident which showed both Dad's bravery and ability to calm agitated soldiers happened in Gulu when an artillery gunman scouted the fast moving Presidential Convoy and leveled his artillery towards the oncoming convoy then he gave the conventional Holuko - HALT! Then the soldier started to harangue his Commander in Chief.

"All the officers have left. We are only soldiers and NCOs. Now you Affende are leaving? Better we die here and now rather than leave you to pass" [sic].

According to Dad, in a hushed tone, he got out of the E 200 Series Merc Coupe and strode towards the 3,000 plus remnants of his Fighting Force and pointed at the daring soldier in reply.

"Here is a soldier. If I had twenty or more like him, we could not be defeated".

This short speech made the soldier hang his head, with tears in his eyes, having realized that he had confronted the Commander in Chief, but the speech had also turned the tide into sympathy from a hostile 3,000 strong battle weary amalgamation of the last Fighting Force.

"Where are the Field Commanders?" Dad asked the soldiers.

"They all headed for Arua" they answered.

"Soldiers, let me go and try and convince them to return to the battle field" interjected Dad.

"We also need reinforcements from Libya and Gulu and Arua Airfield are still in our hands. We will check whether Nakasongola is still in our hands. Kenya has blocked our fuel supply. The only way through is through the Sudan and Libya".

All was lost when Dad got to Arua, for he met with a crescendo of gunfire from soldiers shooting aimlessly. He met with senior officers who sought his audience one by one. He was saddened to hear of the death of Governor Odong of the Chope who was apparently killed by friendly fire - another mystery like that of Godwin Sule in Lukaya.

According to reliable sources, a significant thing happened. Dad finally sought audience with his Minister of Education to whom he handed over the Instruments of Power and asked him to become the President of Uganda. Therefore for all intents and purposes, Brigadier Barnabas Kili was the Interim President of Uganda after Dad was overthrown in 1979 before he handed over the Instruments of Power to the Tanzania Peoples'

Defence Force as a sign of the country having been taken over. It seems Dad kept the Marines Colours and the Army Colours but handed over the Police and the Country's Colours.

CHAPTER FOURTEEN

A special Libyan C-130 Hercules Plane

After Dad arrived in Arua, he continued his feeble broadcasts on the Gilgili Radio Station at Arua. On April 23, 1979, he was still in Arua when a Libyan C-130 Hercules landed at Arua Airstrip right next to his Tanganyika Residence to pick him and several of his associates for the plane trip to Libya. That fateful day, Dad embarked on the outbound journey into exile. He and his entourage left Arua for Libya in a special plane that flew him to Tripoli, Libya where he was reunited with us.

The Russian Embassy had approached him with an ultimatum that if he signed a Pact with the USSR, they would land 25,000 Cubans to restore his regime. The price was Communism. Whether it was beside the point or not, Dad's answer was poignant, for unlike a drowning man who grasps at straws to survive, he told the Soviets "I will not sell a single inch of Ugandan soil just to remain in power. It is my officers who have failed us".

Mzee Doka Bai our Ayivu Elder (Opi) and neighbour in Arua was the last person Dad talked to before he was driven to the awaiting C130 Hercules on his way to Libya. He remembers watching just off our water tank as the plane ascended into the skies.

Dad had told him in passing "I am going to discuss with the Russians in Libya my return. However, if they insist on being the Communist overloads like in Ethiopia then I will not agree to sign, but let the Uganda High Command officers know that they are the ones who failed this country".

"Goodbye my brother" Doka Bai had uttered as the C130 Hercules carrying Dad disappeared into the skies on its way to Libya.

After Dad's departure to go to Libya, there was a lot of aimless gunfire in Arua that night.

On April 23, 1979, Dad had passed by Mzee Doka Bai's house, which is just opposite his water tank on his way to board the C130 plane. He had stopped on a final courtesy call on his neighbour and fellow child of the Okapi for Mzee Doka's mother's maternal uncles were Okapi from Ole'ba in Maracha District.

His friend, brother and neighbour (Dad) had intimated to him, "I am going to get some more reinforcement from Libya but if the Soviets insist that they are in control then I will never allow a single inch of Uganda soil to be under their control. Let it be (wacha na keti basi)".

Dad then put his hands in his pockets and came out with whatever was there but thoughtfully in foreign currency for even he was aware that his 2nd Republic notes were losing value rapidly. He then handed over the dollars to his friend, cousin-brother and neighbour who used to join him in training when he was still the East African Light Weight Champion.

On one of Dad's Annual Leave saunters around Tanganyika Village in Arua, the two were responsible for courting and finally getting Mama Ingi one of Dad's very first concubines in trouble in 1952 when my sister Amina Ingi was born.

Mzee Doka remembered standing, watching towards the northern direction as the C130 took up speed and graciously ascended into the sky with resounding bullets flying around in the Jiako area as soldiers kept firing at anything in total disregard for safety or reason as they expended ammunition. It was as though Dad was being given a 21-gun salute for even one of Doka Bai's brothers shot at some ripe mangoes, setting off a resounding rebuke from his elder brother.

"Why do you have to shoot at the mangoes using that thing? Behave yourself...."

Over the years, Mzee Doka recalled the money his cousin-brother Dad gave him so well for he used it to relocate his family to the Congo (Zaire). He also recounted this story to me when I brought him some money sent by thoughtful relatives of the Al-Amin Family who knew the significance of Mzee Doka Bai to Dad as a neighbour and a relative on his mother's maternal Okapi Lugbara Ethnic group side.

Doka Bai's mother is of the Okapi of Ole'ba, Maracha District. As a Kasanvu (coerced labourer), Mzee Doka of the Ayivu used to get 70 shillings as a Uganda British American Tobacco (BAT) Company Lorry Driver per month. When he joined Grandpa's aunt Asungha's husband's Arua Bus Syndicate Company as a Driver, they paid him 120 shillings per month.

This was in the late forties and mid fifties. The coerced labourers were paid much less. We have to put it in context. They started the Kasanvu scheme around 1919. Therefore 70 cents fit the bill I suppose.

Dad would always send supplies and place them in the hands of Mzee Doka Bai as the Family Quarter Master General, during the Duas, while most errands in the 1960s were the responsibility of the late Shaban of the Lurujo Kakwa clan. Upon his sudden demise, Shaban was later replaced by Alias of the Drimu Kakwa clan. All the above responsibility was taken up by Mzee Sergeant Hussein Diliga post 1979.

Hussein Diliga was the very person who came to pick Joseph and me at Aunt Akisu's homestead in Kayunga, Bugerere when she died in 1970. He was the very person who spied my brother Taban Idoru under the Military Bus seat and took some 20 minutes trying to extricate him from under the seats when he insisted that he wanted to go to Arua with the Funeral Procession of our aunt Akisu. The ultimate errand boy became a Foster Father of sorts replacing Sergeant John Katabarwa.

I don't believe Ugandans and Dad's detractors know that Dad boarded the Hercules plane to Libya penniless but the two countries Libya and Saudi Arabia were generous to him. I was a witness to the amounts he gained from them.

Dad arrived in Tripoli via Benghazi on April 23, 1979 and begun his long life in exile!

Our first days in Libya

In Libya, we were initially placed in a plush residence in downtown Tripoli, which we christened "Palace". The residence had ornate Mediterranean grapevines in the garden and we would spend endless days claiming cars as they crisscrossed a junction right in front of the "Palace" window. "Yangu Eeh Yangu!!!" ("Mine Eeh Mine!!!"), we would scream as the cars sped past the junction. We were then transferred to a Beach Resort called Madina Sahiyah awaiting Dad's arrival.

After Dad was reunited with my siblings and I and the rest of our immediate family, we were all relocated to a government-owned Hotel in Homs, towards the Tunisian border. We were transferred there along with Dad's entourage, which included Ministers, Diplomats, Officers of the Armed Forces and their families.

I recall that Dad arrived in Benghazi on April 23, 1979 from our Arua Tanganyika Aerodrome aboard the C130 Hercules Transporter that Al-Qadhafi sent to pick him up after his government was overthrown. We had a tearful reunion with Dad on April 24, 1979 in Tripoli, Libya.

After we were reunited with Dad, we spent time exploring desert oasis and the famous Roman Coliseum in Homs.

Immediately following our arrival in Libya, Al-Qadhafi in his characteristic generous nature offered to send us all of Dad's children to Malta, which had the second nearest good English schools. Egypt was nearest, but Libya's neighbour was just about to sign a Friendship Treaty with Israel and I guess it had fallen out with its Arab colleagues. By the time Dad arrived on April 23, 1979 after the fall of his government on April 11, 1979, I guess the plan had been sidelined.

An indecent pass by a Libyan Bodyguard

I will never forget the physical fight I started between the D12 ("The Dirty Dozen") as Dad referred to 11 of my brothers and me and a youthful Libyan Bodyguard who made an apparent indecent pass at one of my brothers. The

CHAPTER FOURTEEN

Bodyguard made a pass at my famous brother Moses Kenyi - the one who was allegedly sacrificed and eaten by Dad in 1974! I, the firebrand Tshombe could not stand that so I got into hot water again. I was going to have none of the Libyan Bodyguard's nonsense so I alerted the rest of the D12 ("The Dirty Dozen"). "The Dirty Dozen" included me and my brothers Muhammad Luyimbazi, Hassan Ruba Ali, Yusuf Akisu, Khamis Machomingi, Hussien Juruga Lumumba, Moses Kenyi, Sulieman Geriga, Adam Ma'dira, Issa Aliga, Mao Muzzamil and Abdul Nasser Alemi Mwanga.

    I was first on the scene and instinctively grabbed at the Bodyguard's lengthy hair, demanding to know what he was trying to do. The Bodyguard jokingly tried to get away but the whole bunch of the D12 was on to him and we all started beating the hell out of him. As always, I led the fray and the rest of "The Dirty Dozen" joined me. Our very own Ugandan Bodyguards were the ones who actually stopped us and rescued the Libyan Bodyguard.

    Unbeknownst to us, the Libyan Bodyguard had apparently run upstairs to the second floor, which housed their quarters, to get his AK-47. He had the intention of mowing down President Amin's children but he was restrained and quickly transferred back to the Barracks away from the Hotel complex where we continued to reside.

I still have a framed reprint of a Polaroid snapshot of "The Dirty Dozen" on top of my Pentium Processor and I smile every time I look at the picture as I remember the numerous times we got into trouble. Dad used to laugh about our capacity to get in and out of trouble, as he "taunted" and fondly referred to us as the D12. Nothing came close to the fight involving the Libyan Bodyguard and any mention of that "naughty brawl" always brought about one of Dad's tearful earthquake laughs.

Relocating to the Kingdom of Saudi Arabia

While we lived in Libya, a rift developed between Dad and Al-Qadhafi following Al-Qadhafi's close association with Julius Nyerere while trying to gain the OAU (Organization of African Unity) seat that year 1979. Dad viewed Al-Qadhafi's close association with Julius Nyerere as betrayal. So, in characteristic defiance, he dramatically insisted on walking all the way to Makkah (Mecca) if Al-Qadhafi did not offer him safe passage to the Kingdom of Saudi Arabia.

When Dad felt a year's stay in Libya was long enough for him, he actually walked a distance of almost 5,000+ metres before he was convinced by Ugandan Diplomats, Ministers and his Personal Bodyguards to gracefully return to the hotel complex in the official car. The car had trailed the former Head of State along the whole way. This was the same hotel complex where our family and Dad's entourage had been accommodated from the time Dad landed in Libya after his government was overthrown in Uganda. The Great Libyan Leader finally relented and placed Dad, our family and an entourage of over 80 people on a flight to the Kingdom of Saudi Arabia. So, in 1980 we relocated to Jeddah, Saudi Arabia.

It would be thirty years later in the year 2009 that Al-Qadhafi would finally be elected Chairman of the African Union, which replaced the OAU (Organization of African Unity).

In Jeddah we were first placed at "The Sands" Jeddah. However because of the extensive costs involved in housing an entourage of over 80 people, the Former President's immediate family was allocated a Villa in Makarona, while some of his Ministers and Bodyguards were placed in a Flat complex. This was the same Flat complex that was used as a "ground zero" location to "dupe" the BBC (British Broadcasting Corporation) contingent of Journalist Brian Baron and Muhammed Amin when Dad gave his first Television Interview after the 1979 war.

It is the Building the BBC (British Broadcasting Corporation) contingent of Journalist Brian Baron claimed was Dad's residence in their Article on the first Television Interview Dad gave after the 1979 war. However, we referred to the building as Ujamaa Village.

After residing at "The Sands" Jeddah for a period, some of Dad's Ministers were eventually housed at this location. It was where some of the Bodyguards and Former Ministers Ismail Sebbi and Juma Bashir used to reside before they too were given bungalows in the old quarters in Old Jeddah.

Dad as a devout Muslim and a Training

Much to his credit, once Dad fell silent on the world stage by say 1981, he refocused his energy into understanding further his own religion Islam. For most of the 24 years he lived in exile until his death on August 16, 2003, Dad studied Islam in further depth and he was devoted to and strictly followed the teachings of Islam. During the time several of my siblings and I lived in exile with him, he encouraged us to also devote ourselves to and strictly follow the teachings of Islam.

When we lived in exile, Dad continued demonstrating his unwavering support for Arab People and the Ummah (Community of Muslim Believers). He maintained his close links with the Palestine Liberation Organization (PLO). In fact, he enrolled us the D12 ("Dirty Dozen") as he referred to 11 of my siblings and me, for the Kids'

CHAPTER FOURTEEN

League Commandos Fidayins at the PLO Embassy in Jeddah. The Commando Training through the PLO Embassy in Jeddah was in line with Dad's demand that we understand all forms of combat. In the Commando Training, my favourite move was the Ammam Yakt Tidi. Basically, it is a front mid air flip where one lands with the shoulder blade and feet, while the pelvis is thrust away from the ground!

One eventful day, my cousin Joseph (Yusuf) Akisu brought along his camera and he was taking pictures of us making frontal rolls through a burning metal hoop wrapped with gunny bags and bathed in kerosene when something terrible and scary happened! I had made an initial jump and Yusuf confirmed that it was good but I insisted and wanted to make a second one to bug my younger siblings. They yelled in complaint but I was on a roll. I wanted to show them that I did not fear the fire so I went headlong through the hoop. Unluckily, I kept my legs outstretched too long and I had not knotted them as I executed the somersault. I hit the whole edifice and it came down on me!

I was lucky that our Yemeni Instructor was at hand and he pulled the burning hoop off me. I came out of the fire like a bat out of hell with an instinctive dash towards the sandpit.

All I remember was my brothers' laughter for surely it was hilarious. I rolled in the sand for what it was worth, rubbing sand all over to douse the fire. I still remember my badly singed maroon Adidas Tracksuit.

I suffered second degree burns on my arms and legs. My legacy is a panther like mosaic on my left hand. Somehow after this incident, Dad never let us get back to the Commando Training Camp again. I kept bugging him about it but he let it pass.

Our Boxing and Kung Fu Training

When we lived in exile with Dad, my siblings and I also took up both Boxing and Kung Fu under the stern instructions of a one eyed Palestinian. I recall a time he had a particularly painful way of lumbering up us novices. We would sit cross-legged, then place the soles of our feet together then he would come round behind the novice and forcefully press outwards on each knee, exerting excruciating pain to the pubic tendons. This was supposed to make us flexible, long before I became obsessed with ways Jean Claude Van Damme would make famous in the late eighties. Anyway, at that particular moment, the exercise was particularly painful and hilarious at the same time.

As we sat in a row, the Instructor would enact the punishment as I chose to call it and I, Tshombe would let off a restrained giggle. The one eyed Palestinian Instructor would give me a nasty sidelong glance and inquire, "Why are you laughing? Hmm?"

Sorry sir, I would reply.

I kept up this charade until it came to my turn. The Instructor must have relished the effort when I let off a painful scream and the kids around me were giggling away at my suffering. I must say he reminded us a lot of the famous Bruce Lee. Just to impress us, he would let loose some amazing round the house kicks at the heavy leather bags. I was always overwhelmed by his abilities and always looked back with longing and lament about how my injury at the Commando Training Camp where I suffered second degree burns on my arms and legs stopped us from participating further.

Dad noticed my potential in the Boxing Ring early on and he would sometimes come and show me some moves in the Ring. One particularly devastating move of his was to ask me to stand motionless while he let loose on some particularly close shadow boxing, dead straight at my face. I kept praying to Allah that Dad still had the steady hand, which he proved to have in spite of that omnipotent potbelly.

A Typical day at our household in Saudi Arabia

On a typical day at our household in Saudi Arabia, we had morning prayers at 5:30am. Then at 7:00am, Dad dropped our young siblings Faisal and Khadija at the Expatriates' School, in the family's Caprice Station Wagon. Then he passed by the Safeway to buy groceries. After that, he would begin his extensive phone calls to "dependents" cum political opportunists who kept the flame of his "anticipated return" alive and the phone ringing off the hook in his skeptical ear. They had forgotten that he had told anyone who would hear and understand in Jinja that fateful day on April 12, 1979, "You do not want me now. It's okay. But, But one day you will remember me and you will search for me but you will never find me and you will cry for me Awon'go".

After the phone calls to his "dependents" cum political opportunists, Dad would have lunch at his favourite Pakistani Restaurant and then he would drive off towards the Cornishe for a dip in the sea, having collected our young siblings from school. He would then check on friends like Abdul Rahman, a member of a group they referred to as Arua Boyz or Sheikh Abu Alama and Sheikh Sharif Idris at his Old Jeddah Residence.

Dad had lots of associates with him in Jeddah. Sometimes I would act as their Chauffeur, driving them around Jeddah and neighbouring cities.

Magrib Prayers at 19:00 would find us back home with bags full of groceries for the sagging Freezer and the Frost Free Fridge for the delicate stuff.

Any hint of a malady amongst the kids and Dad would ship the lot of you to King Fahad Military Hospital for an extensive series of check ups. We often joked that Dad spent most of the +26,000 $ US allowance he received from the Saudi Royal Family on medical bills and our education than say on buying the next "Suburban SUV" or even a "Merc" for that matter. He seemed to have made a vow not to look in the direction of that most sought after mode of transportation for it might have reminded him of the past.

Fridays would find us in a long convoy for the Holy City of Makkah Al Mukaramah for Juma Prayers (Friday Prayers) and back to our Al Safa Residence by 19:00 for Magrib Prayers.

CHAPTER FIFTEEN

Our Spiritual experiences in Saudi Arabia

We had a lot of spiritual experiences in Saudi Arabia, the Holy Land of Islam, including entering the Inner Most Sanctuary of the Holy Kaaba. My most spiritual experience took place one eventful day when Dad took us to Makkah on the date when the Governor of Makkah would be doing the annual cleansing of the Holy Site.

As we circulated, which always feels like we are in a Ja'far ("Stream") of people, the Inherent Keeper of the keys to the Kaaba recognized Dad and joyfully grabbed his hand leading him towards the Golden Door up a flight of stairs. Dad instinctively told us to stay close to him as we were given the privilege to enter the Inner Most Sanctuary of the Holy Kaaba. The Keeper of the keys instructed all the boys to pray two Rakkats at each of the four walls of the Kaaba. What struck me was the fact that at every wall and at that particular moment in time, we were facing millions of Muslims from every point of the globe who were praying towards this very centre of the Muslim Universe!

Our Islamic teaching claims that the Kaaba in Makkah is parallel to a similar Kaaba Twaffed in Heaven and that if one were to head straight up from this point, they would actually head up the mythical staircase to heaven.

We were then given the privilege to clean the inside of the Kaaba, which we did with relish and spiritual faith after which we went a final stretch of stairs up to the very top of the Kaaba where brass rings hold the Woven Black Silk Shroud.

The whole family never stopped talking about this event. Whenever I re-tell this story to Learned Imams and Sheikhs in Africa, they always tell me how lucky I was to have had this chance to enter the Inner Sanctuary of the Holy Kaaba.

The significance of the Keeper of the key to the Kaaba recognizing Dad was not lost to me. They had last met in 1972 when Dad came for his initial Haj in the company of the Late King Faisal Bin Abdul Aziz Al-Saud. On that momentous day, as soon as they walked into the Sacred Sanctuary, it started to rain. Shocked, King Faisal Bin Abdul Aziz Al-Saud looked across at his VIP visitor and said, "You must be a special visitor. This last happened centuries ago." Dad had smiled back knowingly because he knew about the renowned rain making skills of his Adibu/Bura Kakwa clan.

Here was Al-Amin being praised for his service to Islam by a descendant of a particular sect appointed by the original Al-Amin (The Prophet Peace Be Upon Him) following the future prophet's just decision in solving a wrangle amongst the Quraish tribe. The tribes were undecided on who was supposed to place the Holy Black Stone on the newly reconstructed Kaaba.

Another highly enlightening experience was Dad's annual ritual of breaking fast at the Haram Alsharif in Makkah from the start to the finish of the Holy Month of Ramadhan. We would set off in a long convoy with him in the metallic blue "Vogue Range Rover" or the white Caprice Classic Chevrolet Estate, while we took the rear in either the burgundy Fleetwood Cadillac or the cream 505 Peugeot Estate. We normally set off right after Asir Prayers and would arrive just before the Magrib Prayers and take up vigil until the announcement to break fast, which we did with dates and fresh fruit juice.

We would then pray in congregation with fellow Muslims, the Magrib Prayers. Then we would go out for a proper supper before returning for the extended Prayer Vigil "Taraweh Prayer" after the Ishah Prayers. We would return to Jeddah before the Morning Prayer and in time to take Suhur/Dako. This ritual would be performed daily for either the 29 or 30 days in the month of Ramadhan.

Dad's immense curiosity was infectious and we would go on extended tours of the Holy Land of Islam and Holy Sites. We almost made it to the top of the famous mountain, which marked the beginning of the Hijrah where Muhammad and Abu Bakr Al Saddiq took refuge from the search by fellow Quraish. Jebel Noor has always been a photo shoot opportunity whenever members of our family came into town. We learnt about and visited Arafat, the site of the final sermon.

A visit in Saudi Arabia from our uncle

I have fond memories of our uncle Baba Ramadhan Dudu Moro Amin Dada. Memorably in 1987 while on a school break, I was given the task of being an Honourary Mutawaf (Guide) for him, with the responsibility of guiding him through a complete Ummrah.

That time, we set off for Makkah as a group comprising the whole family. Then Dad bought tickets on the Domestic Saudia Flight to Madinah - just the two of us. We arrived to a fully packed Harram Al-Shari.

I was able to show my uncle Ramadhan Dudu Moro Amin Dada the Holy Site at the Mimbar where it is recommended to pray two Rakkats since it was highly valued as a site where Arch Angel Jibril would often descend from Heaven to convey the message from Allah. We then joined a long line towards the viewing portal of the graves of Umar, Abu Bakr and Muhammad (Peace Be Upon Him).

CHAPTER FIFTEEN 219

From there, we moved onto a marbled wall where we also prayed two Rakkats since it was also a location where quite often the Arch Angel Jibril would also descend with a message from Allah sub hanah wat Allah. We then moved onto the very first Masjid Al Kubah. From there, we went and visited the battlefield of Uhhud, the burial site of Hammzah Alayhi Sallam.

I showed our uncle the point on the mountain side where at the point of defeat when Khalid Ibn Walid's brilliant military tactics almost cost the Holy Prophet his life, droves of Angels came winging down to earth at that very spot to defend the Holy Prophet. He came out of the attack with a broken tooth and to this day the place is considered close to Heaven as a point of entry and exit for the Holy Angels.

We then went to other points of the steady war front where at a particular location, the Sahabahs had built mosques on the battlefield and they would always pray two Rakkats at each site. I also showed him the mosque at which the commandment came to shift direction from Masjid Al Aqsa towards Makkah and the Holy Kaaba and then went to show him the burial site of the Muhajirin in the centre of Madinah Al Munawarah.

Finally, we set off on a +200 km drive back to Jeddah inside an air-conditioned Kangaroo Spring Hilux Toyota Double Cabin Truck. Sadly, the tour had had some tragic overtone since misleading information had reached us that maybe Mariyam Arube Babirye and Hussien Minari Kato had died. My elder sister Salamssidah and the remaining wife Mama Ariye had probably panicked when sending the information, which turned out thankfully not to be true.

I remember while we were on the flight to Madinah, Baba Ramadhan Dudu Moro Amin Dada suddenly broke down in tears. All I could do was place my hand over his trying to comfort him. The mother of the twins had decided to go back to Uganda leaving the children in Kisangani at the tender age of only four months!

On his hurried way back to Zaire (Congo) on Ethiopian Airlines, I remember the two brothers sitting at the Departure Lounge in an extended heart to heart discussion. What I only found out later on our regular trips for swimming at the Cornishe with Dad was he told me that Baba Ramadhan Dudu Moro Amin Dada had requested Dad to send me to Kisangani to look after him. But Dad had declined claiming that I was still studying in the UK but that when I finished he would think about it.

I always felt touched by that request and in some way my coming to Uganda in 1990 and Baba Ramadhan Dudu Moro Amin Dada's eventful return to his homeland in the early 1990s brought us together again. At the back of his mind he has always had it that I was a very knowledgeable person as far as our religion Islam was concerned which I found amusing.

Running into Nation of Islam's Louis Farrakhan

While we lived in exile in Saudi Arabia, one amazing experience we had was running into Nation of Islam's Louis Farrakhan and his entourage in Saudi Arabia in 1989. The occasion brought back memories of the time in 1975 when Dad invited "Black Empowerment Groups", including the Nation of Islam, Black Panthers, the PLO and other Arab Nationalist Groups to the OAU (Organization of African Unity) Summit in Kampala during the time he was the organization's Chairman. That time, Dad called on the Black Peoples in the American Diaspora to unite and used the occasion of the OAU Summit to implement that agenda.

The day we ran into Louis Farrakhan at the airport in Jeddah, we had escorted my kid brother Moses who was flying back to Paris where he was studying. The way it always happened was that whoever amongst us was next out after a vacation period would receive a formal Kuwerekera (Escort) from Dad and the other siblings.

So, on one of those outward movements, Dad sauntered to the nearest Soda Fountain joint to await departure while we booked in my kid brother Moses, when lo and behold the tiny frame of Louis Farrakhan loomed large with an equally large entourage. I braved myself and approached Louis Farrakhan to pay my respects and he asked where my siblings and I were from. I ventured, Busoga, saw the smiles from my siblings and quickly changed tack, realizing this was a family friend and told him the truth about being from Uganda.

When Louis Farrakhan started rubbing his chin and lamenting that he was leaving but he had wanted to meet Idi Amin again, I winked at my brother Aliga and told the great man to wait just long enough. Shortly after that, Dad approached his good friend, with that familiar great stride with the arms swinging like paddles. What amused us the most was Louis Farrakhan's son who jumped upwards like Atlanta Hawks' Spud Webb for Dad's neck, embracing the giant of a man, who gleefully enjoyed the spectacle. Dad and Louis Farrakhan were then ushered into the VIP Lounge for an extended discussion. That time, Louis Farrakhan also intimated that his daughter and her husband, the Chief of Staff of the Nation of Islam would remain and pay the family a visit.

It was an honour to do the usual run around with our guests. Donna Farrakhan preferred the Popeye Fast Food Restaurant, which had opened a Popeye Branch just off the road to

Sands Hotel where we resided when we first arrived in Jeddah in 1980 while we were used to Kentucky Fried Chicken. I did not realize until later that she had just then acquired 3 Popeye Franchises in the State of Illinois. The Kentucky Fried Chicken Restaurant we frequented was located at the very turn towards Dad's favourite Safeway, which is across the road from Sands Hotel, Jeddah.

    I will never forget how it tickled Leonard Muhammad, Louis Farrakhan's son-in-law and Chief of Staff, to find me listening to MC Hammer. Born Leonard Searcy in 1945, Mr. Muhammad married Donna Farrakhan, Mr. Farrakhan's daughter in 1983 and changed his name to Leonard Farrakhan Muhammad.

    "You like MC Hammer?" queried the Chief of Staff.

    I said I am a discerning dancer and to my mind he is the only one who could beat me in a dance competition.

    "How about Michael?" Louis Farrakhan's Chief of Staff inquired.

    With disgust I frowned and commented Michael can't dance. That is not Soul Dancing, but the Hammer can dance. I also like Bobby Brown but my favourite thung at the moment is the New Jack Swing thung coming from Teddy Riley, I offered in "Black American English".

Muhammad's wife Donna Farrakhan - a cross between Jada Pinket and Beyonce was the leader of the Fruits of Islam Bodyguards no less. I could not help imagining her at our Fidayin Boot Camp in the desert and even dared to ask her.

Your father told us yesterday that you are the Trainer of the Fruits of Islam. I also train and do go through training with the PLO Fidayins, I offered.

Bless her, she blushed but gave a guarded acceptance.

The whole family is light; her mother is an Amer-Indian. So, the blush was obvious. Since the revelations came from her father, I took this chance to ask her to tell her father that Muslim Inc. under Betty Shabbaz and Nation of Islam should make up, for I believe that despite all the misunderstandings, we were in this together, I intimated.

I wonder where she keeps the snapshots we took at the Inter-Continental with the Chief of Staff of the Nation of Islam.

The Nation of Islam dignitaries came to Uganda on Dad's invitation during the OAU (Organization for African Unity) Summit in Kampala in 1975. That year, Dad lined all of us his children at Nile Mansions Hotel (Serena Hotel) and went through a formal introduction of all of us.

I remembered the beautiful bride-to-be who had on the original Whoopi Goldberg beads way before Whoopi showed up on the radar screen and her future husband the bald cameraman. I remembered how she kept asking, with marked wonder, "Are these all your children?" and Dad responding "Yes".

I was at the very end of the row of about 35 children and I could see the bald headed husband to be grinning right next to her. It is funny that I eventually ended up with the very same Isaac Hayes close shaven head.

I asked the Chief of Staff about this golden couple in 1989 when we ran into Louis Farrakhan and his entourage in Jeddah, Saudi Arabia and even Dad was surprised at how I could remember that 1975 occasion. I told him that it was because the groom's "bald head" style is the one I wear today, for they actually got married either in Uganda or Morocco. They actually traversed the country filming and I pray I can get footages and snap shots of their travels. The two lovebirds kept taking photos of the whole Al-Amin brood using expensive cameras - priceless colour photos in 1975.

We got used to Technicolour way back, as per the coloured pictures Dad was fond of taking with his favourite Aluminum Polaroid Camera. That time the Satellite was up and running in Uganda and Dad brought in the earliest versions of Toshiba Colour Televisions - Sony Video decks and the works.

Islam's benign presence in our family

I will provide additional information on the Nubians of Uganda in a subsequent section of the series which along with sections on Grandpa's conversion to Islam and Dad's childhood provide information about the Nubian influence and Islam's benign presence in our family and how my family acquired the Nubian components of our Triad Cultural Heritage. The cultural heritages of Nubian, Kakwa and Anglo-Saxon at heart will be evident throughout the series.

You will recall that Grandpa was converted to Islam by a fellow Kakwa with the title Sultan Ali Kenyi of the Drimu Kakwa clan of Ko'buko (Ko'boko) and my family has had a strong Muslim background ever since. You will also recall that the day Dad was born in 1928, my Grandpa Amin Dada Nyabira Temeresu (Tomuresu) had set off for Eid Al-Adha Prayers amongst the Nubian Muslim Settlement on Kibuli Hill, a suburb of the Ugandan city of Kampala. Dad's brother, my uncle Ramadhan Dudu Moro, who was 9 years old at the time accompanied Grandpa on this day in 1928 that fell on the religious festival Eid Al-Adha which is celebrated by Muslims worldwide. You will further recall that after my grandparents divorced over false allegations that King Daudi Chwa fathered Dad and not Grandpa, Grandma left with Dad to live with her relatives who had retired from the Kings African Rifles and were living in Bombo, Semuto-Luwero, on the outskirts of Kampala.

As I recounted in a previous section, by the time several of my extended family members were discharged from the Kings African Rifles and "settled" as peasants and indentured labourers, the bulk of my family had fully embraced Islam and fully amalgamated with the "Nubi (Nubian) tribe" of Uganda. Many of them had also fully assimilated into the Baganda (Ganda) tribe of Uganda which is how my family became "entangled" with gossiping Ganda and Nubians and caused Dad to be subjected to the Deadly "Paternity Test" on account of Grandma's close relationship with the Ganda Royal Family.

As you also recall, Dad and Grandma lived at Semuto-Luwero for 4 years, from 1937 to 1940 when Dad was between the ages of 9 and 12 years old. During their stay at Semuto-Luwero, Dad studied at the Al-Qadriyah Darasah Bombo (Al-Qadriyah Khanqa, Masgid Noor Bombo), Uganda. He attempted Primary School while at Bombo, sporadically combining this with Garaya [Qur'an Studies].

I have images of the youthful Dad chanting the fantastic voyage of the Holy Prophet's Mihraj (tour to heaven) to a transfixed audience filled to capacity with dignitaries from around the world on an annual Mawlid Ziyarah to Masgid Noor Futuwah in Bombo in the 1930s and 1940s.

By then, Dad was reputed to have attained the level of an adept and he was aware and cultivated a sense of Alam Al Mithal, the mystical world of pure images. Some even claim that Dad's intuition was legendary. He was a renowned seer to some for his eerie ability - a certain ability to foretell future events with amazing accuracy. It was a mystical trait cultivated from his strong association with the Al Qadriyah Order and from having inherited the same ability from his Okapi/Bura mother. Grandma Aisha Chumaru Aate was by far the most revered and powerful member of the "Yakanye Allah Water Movement" at the Fourth Battalion Jinja under the Kings African Rifles. I provide snippets of the "Allah Water Movement" also in a subsequent section of the series.

The Fourth Battalion Jinja under the Kings African Rifles was later converted to the 1st Battalion Jinja under the Uganda Rifles and finally my Dad as Head of State renamed the barracks Al-Qadhafi Garrison. The renaming of the barracks Al-Qadhafi Garrison followed Dad and Al-Qadhafi's Bilateral Joint Declaration on February 14, 1972 between the Great People's Jamahiriya of Libya and the 2nd Republic of Uganda. I write

CHAPTER FIFTEEN

about this Declaration in a previous section of this "Introductory Edition".

From the time Grandpa Amin Dada Nyabira Temeresu (Tomuresu) converted from Catholicism to Islam during the first decade of the 20th Century, the Muslim religion has deeply permeated my immediate family, leading to Dad's strong affiliations with the Muslim Ummah. A case in point was when Dad curtailed his equally strong relationship with Israel in favour of the Muslim Ummah, personified by Muamar Al-Qadhafi of Libya and the Late King Faisal Bin Abdul Aziz Al-Saud of Saudi Arabia, during Dad's rule in Uganda.

The search for my roots and culture was what prompted a passion and hunger in me to begin investigating the various "threads" comprising my "Triad Cultural Heritage". It is also what has encouraged me to uncover Dad's story layer by layer and led me to partner with various individuals interested in Dad's conflicted legacy of hero and villain at the same time. A number of book projects I have embarked on provide the background information for the current project.

I have also embarked on an agenda for Peace, Truth and Reconciliation as outlined in various documents under the Al-Amin Foundation.

About the Author

Margaret Akulia is co-author with Idi Amin's son Jaffar Amin of the book series titled Idi Amin: Hero or Villain? His Son Jaffar Amin and Other People Speak.

www.idiamindada.com

www.ingramcontent.com/pod-product-compliance
Lightning Source LLC
Chambersburg PA
CBHW061637040426
42446CB00010B/1453